Contents

Welcome to Focus on Gender

Welcome to this new publication from the Gender and Development Unit (GADU) of Oxfam. We hope that readers familiar with the GADU Newspack will like the new format and that the publication will reach an even wider constituency in both South and North.

Although there is a growing awareness that relief and development programmes not only affect women and men differently, but also have an impact on gender relations, the situation of poor women continues to worsen, and there is an increasing need to highlight gender in the development debate and document the experience of women.

Focus on Gender has been designed to provide a forum for development practitioners, students and all concerned with the theory and practice of gender-just development, to exchange views, record experience, describe models of good practice, and disseminate information about networks and resources.

Focus on Gender will contain a range of articles, clustered around a particular theme. In the first issue, our guest editor, Geraldine Reardon, has assembled a rich anthology of material on the topic of environment; the June issue will focus on women and violence. Other themes to be addressed in further issues will include income generation and micro-enterprises, North/South co-operation and networking, women and religion, and gender issues in emergencies.

We have no readers' letters in this first issue but look forward to hearing your reactions both to the style and content and hope that it will become a medium for dialogue and debate. The book reviews, further reading list, and 'News from GADU' have been compiled to promote networking and information sharing. We hope that future issues may include a 'noticeboard' with information from readers around the world.

Women in the South and the North are challenging the structures which subordinate them. In *Focus on Gender* we hope to record some of those challenges and develop a vision of development which does justice to all, both women and men. We welcome your help in this endeavour.

BRIDGET WALKER, GADU

Editorial

Geraldine Reardon

THIS FIRST ISSUE of *Focus on Gender* looks at environment. Contributions come from different parts of the world and deal with different experiences of 'environment'. Some of the articles tell harrowing stories of the effects of environmental disaster and degradation. Women express anger at the treatment of women by environment 'experts'. There is little to be cheerful about in the environment issue itself, but there is hope in reading how women in the most desperate circumstances are looking to the future and organising to take control of their space in the environment.

To begin to understand what gender and environment means, we should look to the late Joan Davidson's overview of the close and complex relationships of many women in the South with their surroundings. This is a sound introduction to the wide range of issues and situations linking women and the environment. Women are profoundly affected by environmental degradation, but to understand how this happens it is necessary to look at underlying factors such as debt and structural adjustment, trade, aid, war and social structure.

The issue of access to land and land rights comes up in many of the contributions. Few women own the land they work on and therefore do not always benefit from environmental improvements. Its degradation does affect them — as the land

deteriorates so do the resources available to them and the harder they have to work for smaller rewards. Land rights and land reform are environmental issues for women but they are rarely identified as such by environmental experts, or by politicians. The fact of the widespread marginalisation of women in society, the law and economic life, still needs to be addressed by those who want to 'save' the environment from the people who depend on it most.

In this issue Judy Adoko expresses her fierce indignation at the apparent assumption by development workers in Uganda that rural women using wood for fuel are showing a careless disregard for the 'environment'. Her explanation of the situation shows how women and their work are reduced to being demonstration projects for visitors while those controlling the commercialisation of firewood are ignored. It is clear that here, as elsewhere, a chasm in understanding exists between local women and the environmental and development experts.

Rural women are not unaware of the concept of environmental degradation but their choices are limited and their responses might appear to an outsider to be less than ideal. Under closer scrutiny their choice might prove to be a sensible course of action, given the constraints they have to work within: they make the most of what they have today because that is all they have. Poor people, often women, use finite resources — fuelwood, fish, water — out of necessity, not because they seek an easy short-term option at the expense of their children's future.

Removing the causes of women's poverty has to be part of the solution for environmental stability.

Rural women want to play a part in sustaining the natural environment but they cannot embark on schemes which jeopardise their immediate, very precarious livelihood. There has to be some assurance that they will not lose what they have worked so hard for. Removing the causes of women's poverty has to be part of the solution for environmental stability.

Judy Adoko's point that women's time and energy is often assumed to be unlimited is taken up by Irene Guijt in her outlineof new training materials for natural resource management fieldworkers — *Women on Earth*. She states that there is an assumption that 'women's active participation in natural resource management projects will be automatic, regardless of whether there will be any direct benefit for them in doing so'. Understanding how people work and why they use the methods they do is an early step in developing a way of working together. Adopting a gender perspective must be part of this understanding.

Joanne Harnmeijer and Ann Waters-Bayer describe how environmental degradation affects the health of rural women farmers by creating more work for little reward, and yet how women's health can also be undermined by projects which increase agricultural production. Children then become even more necessary, to help with the heavier burden of work; but giving birth to and caring for children becomes an additional drain on the mother's time, energy and health.

Increasing consumption of natural resources is the reason given by many prominent defenders of the environment for identifying 'over-population' as the key culprit in environmental degradation. But this is often a false perception, and the charge is made without examining their own society's part in resource consumption, and with little regard for the daily needs of poor women. A strongly worded statement from DAWN refutes this analysis and points to changes to be made at a world level to promote sustainable development and ease the burden on women.

The pressures of the system of international trade and increasing industrialisation have intensified not only hazards to the natural environment but hazards in the workplace. Around the world local economies are being transformed by the development policies of government and international institutions. People are deserting their rural homes for the towns and cities. As the cost of living escalates and as land deteriorates or is closed to them, they seek a new ways to survive.

In sub-Saharan Africa women have been forced by drought and the rapidly declining economic situation to join the ranks of male migrants to urban centres. Here they face new types of environmental problems — inadequate housing and sanitation, disease and industrial pollution. In Senegal, for example, women and their children are struggling to make a living without even having a home. Mariam Dem describes projects which are trying to enable women to earn money while maintaining their home base. She knows this is not the only solution and calls for more research to find out what women's real needs are and how they can be adequately met.

In other parts of the world — South-East Asia and the Americas — economies such as Mexico are being transformed by export-led policies of industrialisation. Women are leaving rural areas in search of work to earn money in the new cash economy.

Agricultural land is being turned over for new factories, without the necessary supporting sanitation or social services. Towns are growing up around industrial sites in which most of the employees are women, exploited because of their low social status. Industrial waste is rarely controlled properly so that many of the processes which cause occupational health problems in the factories can be directly linked to severe illnesses and death in the community.

The plantation system is not new, and it has never been a safe working environment, but with the introduction of agri-chemicals the hazards are even greater. Research by PAN and by Tenaganita in Malaysia has shown that women plantation workers are given the most dangerous jobs. Direct contact with chemical pesticides seriously affects their health and that of their unborn children. In addition to carrying out more research in other countries in Asia, PAN are holding a series of training workshops to help local organisations combat the use of pesticides. The Serdang Declaration reflects their concern with an entire system of production and consumption.

In an environmental disaster, women can be more vulnerable than men. Disasters present particular dangers for women which can be related directly to their social position. It is not just the cruel climate which devastates lives but the cruelty of social systems which create barriers to survival. In disasters which strike suddenly and without warning many women are trapped in the homes which they fear leaving; they risk their own lives to save their children; and afterwards they are prevented from receiving their fair share of relief aid. At the same time images of suffering women are cynically used to raise funds for relief programmes.

Rasheda Begum describes with anger and bitterness the treatment of women in Bangladesh following the horrific cyclone of 1991. She tells how women's lives were lost because of social conventions, and how the needs of women were ignored during the relief work. She describes the discrimination and obstruction she met as a relief worker. Determined that women should not be treated like this in future, she lists changes which need to be made to disaster relief programmes.

In an environmental disaster, women can be more vulnerable than men.

Other environmental disasters do not come suddenly but are agonisingly slow. The psychological effects of living in a serious drought cannot be underestimated. The stress caused by the burden of extra work, of daily hunger and death, and of not knowing when it will end, can be compounded by the pain of abandonment. From Zambia, Nawina Hamaundu tells how women, whose husbands deserted them to remarry in an area where there was still food, continue to find ways of coping. Throughout Southern Africa, despite the gnawing hunger, women are finding new personal strength and are organising for new strategies.

Environmental degradation has many hidden victims. When a fishery dies the first response is to think of the fishermen who are without work and to mourn their loss of a way of life. In most small-scale fishing communities women are also directly dependent on the resource for their livelihood and their status. It is women who control the processing and marketing of the fish, and whose earnings support the family. The case of Laguna Lake in the Philippines is replicated thousands of times around the world as subsistence fisheries are destroyed by outside intervention and industrial pollution. When the resource dies the women, as well as the fishermen, must also find ways of coping with the loss of their way of life. A loss of autonomy — from an independent business women to a laundress — can also bring a loss of self-esteem. Fisherwomen, such as those at Laguna Lake have not given up and are organising to regain their lost position.

What is environment and why is it important for women? It is not just rainforests, wild birds, and holes in the ozone layer; it is also where people live and work. Their relationship with the environment is determined by their social position and by the work they do. Definitions of environment and prescriptions for solutions to environmental problems are dangerous without understanding the specifics of each case. As Nanneke Redclift says, global needs are not unitary and self-evident.

In programmes for sustainable development, experience has shown that a high level of sensitivity is necessary if development is to be first acceptable and then sustainable. It is important to know what women and men each mean by environment and what the environment means to them. Gender is a variable in environmental analysis because men and women occupy different spaces, carry out different work, have different responsibilities and different needs.

The concept of environment has appeared in recent history as if it were something just invented. For the vast majority of the world's population 'environment' is not a new concept but a basic fact of life. Poor women, in the countryside and in the cities, live and work close to their environment — whether on a small farm, a plantation, in an urban community, or in an industrial zone. Problems of food, energy, sanitation and health confront them directly wherever they live and work. This is their environment.

Farmers on Sabu Island, Indonesia. Women in most Southern countries are at the centre of subsistence food production. JEREMY HARTLEY/OXFAM

Women's relationship with the environment

Joan Davidson

Adapted from 'Women and the Environment', paper written for the Third Meeting of Commonwealth Ministers Responsible for Women's Affairs. Ottawa, Canada, 9-12 October 1990.

IT IS DIFFICULT to define quite where 'environment' begins and ends for women in developing countries. Almost all development activities in some way affect their surroundings — especially in rural areas. Changes in agriculture, forestry, and water and waste management all have local environmental implications which affect women. Women are also directly affected by specifically 'environmental' activities — those designed to rehabilitate degraded areas, reduce pollution or conserve genetic variety.

The way in which women relate to a number of different natural resources, in both rural and urban areas, are explored briefly below. The analyses show how and why women's interests have been damaged, and how they have responded to environmental crises.

Women and land

Cultivable land is the basic resource for meeting food needs and often for servicing livelihoods. Women are at the centre of subsistence food production — accounting for more than 80 per cent in some African countries. Women also produce cash crops, both on their own account, and as hired labour on commercial and family farms.

Yet, according to UN statistics, women own no more than one per cent of the world's land, and even where they have access to it for farming, their tenure is often costly and uncertain. Without ownership of land or secure access to it, women are denied access to credit, training, and other supports to production, and cannot engage in the long-term conservation practices they have traditionally used.

In spite of agrarian reforms in many developing countries, most productive land remains in the hands of relatively few people — the commercial (mainly male) producers. Under formal and informal resettlement programmes, poor women have either become landless, or been forced onto the less productive areas where yields are lower and output is of poorer quality. Attempts to grow subsistence crops in highly marginal environments — on land which may be unstable, dry or subject to waterlogging, pest-ridden and disease-prone — result in severe soil erosion and the related destruction of water and forest resources. Thus begins a cycle of accelerating impoverishment — of people and the environment. Poor farmers may over-exploit land and, as fallow periods shorten, the potential for soil recovery is reduced. Scarcity of fuelwood results in the burning of crop and animal wastes, formerly used to maintain soil fertility. Crop yields, the cooking of food, and diets may all deteriorate.

Green Revolution agriculture — a development 'success' of the 1970s — has bypassed the problems of women farmers. Intensive food production with hybrid, high-yield seed varieties, like intensive production of other cash crops for export, has been beyond the reach of most women farmers, who have no capital for the inputs required such as machines for planting and harvesting, irrigation, pesticides, and the hybrid seeds themselves.

Made landless or pushed in to marginal

Women and women's groups are in the forefront of experiments in sustainable agriculture.

environments, women have to feed families from smaller and more impoverished plots; they may also work (often unpaid) as labourers in cash-crop farming. The work burdens of this 'double' day are exacerbated by the need for women to travel greater distance to collect fuelwood, water, fodder and food when the environment deteriorates as a result of intensive farming. In the Indian state of Rajasthan, now on the brink of a desertification disaster, wells and once-flowing rivers are dry. In 1975, the World Bank and its partners supported the introduction of irrigated cash cropping of sugar cane. In an area with just 60 centimetres of rainfall annually, the cultivation of sugarcane has caused groundwater levels to fall dramatically. The water table is now too low to support regular subsistence cropping.

Evidence is abundant that highly-mechanised, chemical-fed agriculture, often dependent upon large-scale irrigation regimes, damages soil fertility, surface water and groundwater resources, and tree cover. Locally, heavy use of pesticides has increased pest immunity and brought

greater infestation, while species diversity has declined. This has reduced the capacity of subsistence farmers to adapt to changing weather patterns by selecting the more resilient seeds. This has also meant that the rich fund of species knowledge (held by women) is being progressively lost.

Thus, not only have the benefits of intensive agriculture bypassed women, but they have suffered, directly and indirectly, from its 'success'. Their self-reliance and their capacity to sustain the environment are undermined.

Women and women's groups are in the forefront of experiments in sustainable agriculture such as introducing more flexible cropping patterns, widening species diversity, recycling organic nutrients, and other techniques for long-term resource conservation. Traditional methods of interplanting and crop rotation are blended with new styles of agroforestry to provide an alternative approach which combines environmental improvements with direct development gains for women.

Clearly, such innovations do not remove the injustices of land distribution and other inequities that women farmers face. But sustainable agriculture projects can often be the trigger for other improvements initiated by the farmers themselves — crop innovation, for example.

Women and water

In many areas, women are 'invisible' water managers, responsible for supplying the water needs of the family, domestic animals and sometimes agriculture. A number of studies have shown how their role in searching for potable supplies and carrying water over long distances is important for the health, economy, and social development of local communities. Yet women are frequently excluded from the planning, implementation, and maintenance of water supplies. At the same time, they suffer the consequences, as in Rajasthan, of intensive, commercial logging, agri-cultural development, migration and resettlement, and cutting for firewood and charcoal — have environmental consequences which im-pinge directly upon the lives of poor women. Work burdens are increased as they must forage further to find fodder, water, and fuel, leaving less time available for income generation and other activities to im-prove their standards of living.

Women are usually responsible for supplying the water needs of their family, domestic animals and crops. This task is physically demanding and sometimes hazardous, as here in Bihar, India.

ACHINTO BHADRA/OXFAM.

Women's work — in the home, on the land and in small industries — depends much more than men's upon biomass energy, especially wood. Less wood means women may reduce cooking times, with the consequence that they and their children eat poorer food, sometimes dangerously undercooked. It also means that crop and animal wastes, normally used to maintain soil fertility, become substitutes; but they are inefficient, polluting household fuels. Higher prices for imported fuels and the commercialisation of fuelwood to serve rural (and increasingly, urban) markets have further increased the pressures upon women's traditional supplies of wood as a 'free good'. The Food and Agriculture Organisation predicts that 2,000 million people will suffer acute fuelwood shortage by the end of the century.

The extension of commercial forest management, with clear felling, the replanting of ecologically damaging species and the exclusion from decision-making of the affected local groups, have denied women

irrigated agriculture and, elsewhere, of polluting industries.

Women, forests and energy

Forests play a special role in the lives of poor women. Not only are trees important in protecting watersheds, regulating water flows and maintaining soil fertility and air quality, but they provide a 'cornucopia' of benefits — food, fodder, fuel, building materials, medicines and many of the materials for women's income-earning activities.

Increasing rates of deforestation — from

In Burkina Faso, 90 per cent of energy needs are met from wood. Increasing deforestation makes the task of gathering fuelwood more difficult and time-consuming.   MARK EDWARDS/OXFAM

access to their forest life-support systems.

Women have also suffered from well-meaning but inappropriate development activities. Some social forestry schemes, for example, with their emphasis on eucalyptus and other commercially valuable species, have ignored women's interests, not only by excluding them from the benefits, but in other ways, by diverting scarce resources, such as water, to be used as inputs to the schemes.

The Chipko movement and similar groups show how women have fought not only to protect forests but to rehabilitate them and introduce successful new tree-planting initiatives.

Women in urban environments

Poor women who have migrated to urban environments also face problems of deteri-orating health, environmental degradation, and resource depletion, often more acutely than their rural sisters. Most live as squatters in the centres of cities or in the unplanned informal settlements on their margins. These squatter settlements are often built on land unfit for housing, prone to landslides, flooding, or pollution from industry. There are few, if any, services: no regular water supply, sewerage, garbage removal, or electricity. Roads and transport facilities are poor, medical care and education inadequate or absent.

Women, especially, suffer from three kinds of environmental degradation in these urban-fringe areas. The effects of minimal services, the constant danger of industrial pollution, and the cumulative deterioration of the urban hinterland. Around most cities in developing countries (as around large refugee camps), waste disposal, deforestation, overcropping and overgrazing have so damaged soils that erosion, flooding or desertification has followed.

In spite of some progressive schemes, the special needs of women are still ignored in many housing projects which are designed to improve informal settlements through upgrading or site-and-service schemes. House designs and plot sizes take no account of women's need to care for children, grow food or earn an income. Nor are women yet adequately represented in low-income housing management.

The underlying factors

In all these expressions of women's relationship with the environment, the problems are underpinned by the deteriorating economic circumstances of developing countries. Foremost among these are low rates of growth, high international interest rates and unsustainable debt-service burdens, declining terms of trade, and the responses of structural adjustment which have led to more export-led cash cropping at the expense of food security, and reductions in spending on health, education, training, and other services upon which women depend. While there is no detailed evidence of the effects of structural adjustment on women's environmental interests, the local consequences of intensive cash cropping and forest exploitation clearly penalise them. Higher prices for food and energy may force women to abandon traditional conservation practices and degrade fragile ecosystems. Higher prices for imported fossil fuels prevent any switch away from wood fuel and increase pressures upon dwindling forest resources. Adverse terms of trade, especially low and unstable commodity prices, have hit women producers as well as men.

Declining flows of official development assistance to developing countries and the resulting net resource transfers from them, the tying of aid to large-scale and industrial development projects, the failure of aid projects to address the needs of the poorest, and adverse environmental consequences, all rebound upon women.

Rapid population growth, apart from increasing environmental stress because of greater pressure on natural resources, is a further drain upon women's capacity for effective environmental management. Repeated pregnancies coupled with inadequate diets and the burdens of caring for small children all drain women's physical energy.

Locally, the lack of other support mechanisms combine to limit women's effectiveness as resource managers. Without title to land, they have no access to credit for farm improvements, conservation measures, energy-saving technologies or the development of viable income-generating enterprises. Often women are discriminated against in the content and style of training available, including extension advice. Foreign technologies and policies advocated by external agencies are often inappropriate and fail to build on women's traditional knowledge and practices of natural resources conservation. There are excellent examples of women's groups taking action to provide alternatives. But these initiatives reach relatively few women.

Conflict prevents any long-term investment in conservation measures.

Continuing conflicts between and within states have devastating environmental consequences and women are frequently hard hit, as they are presently in Ethiopia, Mozambique, and elsewhere in Africa. Conflict prevents any long-term investment in conservation measures. Refugee camps grow and with them their degraded, treeless hinterlands.

Without action on all the underlying factors — debt and structural adjustment, trade, aid, population growth, discrimination in local support mechanisms and civil conflict — women's efforts to resist environmentally damaging policies and to restore and protect the status of women will be decisive for the protection of the environment and natural resources.

References

Cecelski E (1987) *Linking Energy with Survival*; International Labour Office, Geneva.

Commonwealth Expert Group on Women and Structural Adjustment (1989) *Engendering Adjustment for the 1990s*; Commonwealth Secretariat, London.

Gubbels, P A and Iddi, A (1986) *Women farmers: cultivation and utilization of soybeans among West African women through family health animation efforts*; World Neighbours, Oklahoma City.

Shiva, V (1989) *Staying Alive — Women, Ecology and Development*; Zed Books, London.

Joan Davidson

Joan Davidson, Oxfam's policy advisor on environment and development, died on 21 October. Her untimely death is a tragic loss to Oxfam and the wider movement campaigning for more sustainable development. She did pioneering work in raising awareness of the gender dimension of environment and development issues, resulting in the publication, with Irene Dankelman, of *Environment and Women in the Third World* (1988).

In April 1990 she joined Oxfam's Public Affairs Unit, and with her job-share partner, Dorothy Myers, co-authored *No Time to Waste: Poverty and the Global Environment*. The book was launched to coincide with the United Nations Conference on Environment and Development. Joan lobbied to get issues of poverty, gender and small-scale, community-based solutions onto the Rio agenda, and with her colleague, Tricia Feeney, represented Oxfam on the official UK delegation at UNCED.

She was a brilliant and creative thinker and writer on a variety of subjects, including greening the inner cities and wider planning issues. Joan had a holistic approach to life and was an admirable teacher and enthusiast. She was a perfectionist, driven by her passionate concern for people and her desire to bring about change — whether in the inner cities in Britain or rural villages in the Third World.

She leaves a husband and two sons, and a wide circle of friends. Those of us who have had the privilege of working with Joan will sorely miss her creative energy and her drive.   DIANNA MELROSE

Environmental change and quality of life

Joanne Harnmeijer and Ann Waters-Bayer

How do farmers see environmental changes affecting their family's well-being? How are they try-ing to cope with and improve the situation? What can outsiders do to support them in these efforts? These questions were addressed in the March 1992 issue of ILEIA Newsletter, a journal of the Information Centre for Low External Input in Sustainable Agriculture. The following is an edited version of that issue's editorial.

IN Participatory Technology Devel-opment (PTD), the farmers choose the options they would like to explore. In technology assessment, the farmers judge whether the results of the PTD process suit their circumstances. Their choice of options — whether with low or high levels of exter-nal inputs, whether for more or less sus-tainable forms of farming, will be based to a large extent on how they see changes in their environment, their constraints, and their opportunities. Their assessment will be based on what they value in life — and this is much more than merely increased yields from crops and animals.

Although assessment of sustainability demands that more levels be taken into account than just the farm level, we have chosen to focus first on farmers' views of changes in their environment. Have these changes affected their health in the very wide sense of 'well-being' or 'quality of life'?

Coping, adapting, improving

Throughout the world, people are well aware of environmental change. They are coping with it. They are adapting to it. In the face of constant change, they are trying to create a better life according to their val-ues. If would-be development agents are sincere in their desire to participate in peo-ple's grassroots development projects, then they must find ways of recognising what people are trying to do — and support these efforts.

When the people's views are sought — and when their initiatives are recognised — there is no room for the pessimistic fore-casts often made by environmentalists. Oral histories from the Sahel,[1] for example, testify to people's versatility and ability to adapt in the face of considerable odds. For example, a decrease in per capita wood consumption does not necessarily indicate a woodfuel crisis; instead, it may indicate how women very sensibly respond to decreased woodfuel supplies by improving the way they use firewood.

Relieving women's burdens

Besides oral histories, various other tech-niques of participatory rural appraisal — rapid or otherwise — can be used effective-ly to stimulate local people to express their views about the implications of environ-mental change for their quality of life.

As increasing time is spent on collecting or economising on water and fuelwood, less time is available for improvements in agricultural production. Yet, as the wife of a 'model farmer' in Kenya showed, intensification of farming is making even more demands on women's time.

This is also an issue which has to be squarely addressed in designing and assessing innovations in low-external-input and sustainable agriculture (LEISA). Low-external-input may mean high-internal-input of labour — often by women. By focusing on this problem now, we hope that future research will pay particular attention to the demands which LEISA technologies make on women. The next obvious step then is to work together with women to develop technologies which relieve, rather than increase, their workload.

Why women get tired

Environmental degradation affects women in many ways, especially when they have primary responsibility for producing food for the family. As supplies become scarcer and of poorer quality, getting food and fuel takes more time, thus having a direct impact on the time available for food production within the household, and on the nutritional status and health of household members. Water shortages, declining soil fertility, and fuel shortages are all part of inter-linked circuits of shortages begetting shortages: less water means fewer crops — less fodder means fewer livestock — less dung means poorer crops, and so on.

Not only do agricultural crops suffer, wild plants which farming families collect to supplement family nutrition, to use as medicines, and sometimes also to sell, disappear. Poorer-quality fuels are burned for cooking and heating, causing more smoke and, thus, more ailments of the eyes and respiratory tract. And, at the end of the day Ma has to work harder and longer.

This chain of cause and effect should be obvious, but what is less obvious is that **increased** production from farming can also lead to poorer nutrition and health. This is the case when cash crops or 'modern' foods are promoted to the extent that they replace traditional foods. Then the farming family buys or grows foods which are often less various and nutritious than the traditionally grown and gathered foods. Agriculture with chemicals may give higher yields, but what about residues in and on food or pollution of (drinking) water?

A further important but complex relationship between environmental degradation and health concerns family size. As Caldwell[2] points out, decisions about family size can, to a large extent, be explained by the nature of the household economy. When more labour is needed to derive a living from a degraded environment, more

Pounding grain, Senegal. Many of the household tasks carried out by women are physically exhausting. Deteriorating environments mean women have to work even harder.

BERNARD TAYLOR/OXFAM

children are needed to supply this labour. The draining effect of numerous pregnancies and child births and the demands on women's time, energy and health of caring for small children are multiplied by the increasing difficulties of obtaining water and fuelwood.

First needs first

It is therefore not surprising that, when agricultural development workers attempt to support farmers' efforts to improve their situation, the first priority may not be to improve farming techniques. This was encountered by World Neighbors in Togo, where rural communities chose to improvewater supply and eradicate the water-related disease Guinea worm, so that they would be able to work their fields.

It is important that development projects address a wide range of farmers' needs, and not only identify felt needs, but also respond to local people's ideas of how to address them.

Outsiders must also realise that, in the motivation for and process of farmers' efforts to adjust to changing circumstances, aspects of culture and identity can be very important. Farmers assess new technologies not only according to economic costs and benefits but also according to the effects of innovations on physical and spiritual well-being.

Whose quality of life?

When talking about environmental management by local people trying to ensure their livelihood, the wider political dimensions cannot be ignored. First of all, the affected communities need to make their plight — and their achievements — more widely known. This may serve to obtain financial and moral support from influential people.

Publicity may also be a way to exert public pressure to prevent policies being implemented which are detrimental to the environment and health of farming communities. In Thailand, the journalist Sanitsuda Ekachai and the Thai Development Support Committee have publicised a policy aimed at protecting health by fighting narcotics. The deforestation and high levels of pesticide use associated with growing cabbages in place of opium poppies is having devastating effects on vegetation and water supply and thus, on the well-being of local farmers. What is good for some, is bad for others.

It is important that development projects address a wide range of farmers' needs, and respond to local people's ideas of how to address them.

Conflicts of interests also arise when measures proclaiming nature conservation bring benefits only to a privileged segment of the population. Cases from South Africa quite forcefully bring out the political struggle of communities threatened with measures that uproot their environment and themselves from land they have used for centuries.

Only when individuals and communities join forces can they hope to have some impact on the power game that would otherwise ignore the rights of local residents.

1 Cross N and Barker R (eds) (1991) *At the desert's edge: oral histories from the Sahel*, SOS Sahel/Panos, London
2 Caldwell J (1982) *Theory of Fertility Decline*, Academic Press, London

Further reference:
Cecelski E (1987) 'Energy and rural women's work: crisis, response and policy alternatives', *International Labour Review* 126(1):41-64

Sustainable development: women as partners

Mariam Dem

This article has been edited from a paper presented by Mariam Dem at the ICVA Forum March 1991, Dakar, translated by Sarah Perman and Tim Beech.

THE 1980s saw southern Saharan Africa plunge into an unprecedented economic crisis. In countries such as Senegal the essentially rural economy, dependent as it is on the vagaries of climate and fluctuating exchange rates, was severely weakened. Agriculture expanded only slightly and food production failed to keep pace with the accelerated population growth. Food needs were not met by domestic production.

In order to break out of this spiral of decline governments turned to external borrowing — US$134 billion in 1988, according to a World Bank report on sub-Saharan Africa. Instead, the economic crisis became entrenched by the continued build-up of foreign debt.

In addition, IMF-imposed Structural Adjustment Programmes in the region, initiating liberalisation of the economy and privatisation of state services, have led to weak economic growth, or sometimes to no economic growth at all, and to a decline in living conditions. In the urban environment it is leading to a situation of misery on a scale never seen before. Social indicators are reaching the danger point as poverty spreads and grows deeper.

One adjustment after another has led to widespread disillusionment; people no longer believe that their living conditions will ever improve.

Poverty in the urban areas

Inappropriate economic policies, such as Senegal's New Agricultural Policy, have exacerbated the deterioration in living conditions by advocating the liberalisation of the agricultural sector, in particular the abolition of state subsidies for agricultural inputs. In desperation, the rural population of Senegal are leaving their rural villages in search of food, money, and greater dignity.

In *L'Etat du Tiers Monde* (1989) Noel Cannat notes that the population of sub-Saharan Africa is increasing at four times the rate of the world population. Senegal is typical of this phenomenon.

In the urban centres, the quality of life is also deteriorating. Thirty-nine per cent of this still primarily agricultural economy now live in towns. The urban population is growing rapidly as a result of the natural increase in the population at a rate of 2.7 per cent per year, and the massive exodus of population from the rural areas.

The state, once the leading employer, is getting rid of its employees through the so-called 'voluntary redundancy programme' and is no longer recruiting new staff; it is abandoning those companies it used to support, ending state aid to commercial enterprises, and cutting back on social investment. In 1989, 30,000 officials were sacked from rural employment agencies, and investment in social programmes has been drastically reduced. Businesses and factories are shutting down or laying-off most of their staff. Unemployment is rife.

Women and the economic crisis

Women are particularly affected by this crisis, both in the countryside and in the towns, each situation posing its own set of problems. The increase in poverty in countries such as Senegal has also led to the feminisation of the population: men are leaving Senegal for work and studies elsewhere, so that now 3,618,000 of the 7,171,000 Senegalese are women.

The unemployment created by reduced public spending puts the burden of bringing in an income for the whole family more heavily on women than ever before. In the countryside, the fall in the price of cash crops means that women have to do extra work in order to increase production on their own land. This increased workload does not in itself mean an increase in women's income because the women do not always control this land — in most cases it is controlled by men.

In urban areas, the increase in housing costs forces women and their children into poor housing conditions. Unemployment has increased the burden on women of making ends meet for the family. They are turning to the informal sector — a wide range of services and small-scale manufacturing — to keep the family going.

However, this increased role for women in the struggle for economic survival has not changed their position within the community. They continue to be exposed to all forms of discrimination in everyday life. In the urban areas, as in the countryside,

Market traders, Senegal. Women are increasingly turning to the informal sector to bring in an income to keep their families going. Diane Crocombe/Oxfam

power remains firmly male: land rights, family law, access to credit, access to technology, and access to education. As a consequence of the socio-cultural environment, the effects of the economic crisis in urban areas hit mainly women, and limit their opportunities to improve the physical environment.

To tackle misery and destitution, disadvantaged populations everywhere put survival strategies into action. In Senegal women play the greatest part in these. Nothing is beyond them: they are prepared to undertake any work as long as it brings in a little income to help feed their family and pay for the education of their children. Many are fortunate in still having their traditional associations to rely on and to work within, and where possible they readily align themselves with these organisations to benefit from development activities.

Sustainable development for urban women

Oxfam intends to give more support to the urban women who have been badly affected by Senegal's economic crisis. It plans to do this by participating in the movement people are creating to free themselves from poverty.

Support has been given to women from urban areas in their attempts to organise themselves and to carry out income-generating activities. This support has assumed different forms — the most important of which is to place funds at the women's disposal for carrying out activities which bring in an income to enable them to improve their own and their families' lives.

Another form of support has been in backing women's organisations so that they can act as a counter-balance to women's exclusion from the spheres of influence which affect their lives, and to their marginalisation, which is often linked to their lack of information and training.

In sum, our work with women in urban

areas aims to support them in the context of sustainable development, by promoting and strengthening organisations which mobilise women to earn a living, to improve their health and education, and to learn about and defend their rights.

Above all, however, our task is to further a process of change through support which answers women's needs by financing income-generating activities to give women more economic power; improving their livelihood by promoting education, health and the preservation of the environment; and supporting grassroots initiatives in the rural population in order to slow down the drift to the cities.

Some examples of women working together

A group of Serere women (the Serere are Senegal's second ethnic group) have settled in the capital, Dakar, having left their villages to follow their husbands. The women wanted to maintain solidarity by becoming organised. Credit funds have enabled the women to support their small trading activities without being at the mercy of moneylenders, nor being forced to abandon their family through a lack of money, as is so often the case.

This support has also consisted of training which sensitises women to family planning. This is in response to the distress of those women who, with nine or ten children, are faced with health problems and enormous difficulties in finding food and lodging.

Another group are the 'pounders of Castor', rural women who came to Dakar during the dry season to earn an income for their families by pounding millet and then selling the hulled grain in competition with large-scale traders. Unfamiliar with the city, most had no base in the town and so would sleep with their small children in the market under very difficult conditions.

Oxfam aims to 'root' these women in

their villages by financing their work during the long nine months of the dry season. The women work not only in millet trading, but also in sheep-fattening and other agricultural activities.

Working with women for sustainable development

Sustainable development for women means there are problems to be tackled:

- Access to the ways and means of production such as land, agricultural equipment and inputs: in Senegal, women do not generally have any land, despite the law which administers land as the national estate, accessible to all. The custom of patriarchal control of the land means that women and their organisations often are given land which is not wanted because it is either too far away or barely fertile.

- Insufficient and inaccessible resources for women: because women are far from the centres of decision-making, criteria for the allocation of resources ignore women's circumstances.

- The absence of information and training: women need to be able to apply their own choices and manage their lives in the best possible way.

- The need to strengthen the space for women's independent reflection and expression: often bound by their socio-cultural and political environments, women, particularly those from the poor sections of society, often accept what is suggested to them because they have not been given the opportunity to say what they want or are able to do.

Mariam Dem (right) talking to an Oxfam-supported women's group. Support for women who are organising themselves can help create and strengthen women's confidence. JEREMY HARTLEY/OXFAM

Questions to ask ourselves

Like many development NGOs, most of our work is carried out in rural areas. We are now asking ourselves questions about the realities of life for urban women. Strategies and techniques which have been successful in rural areas are not necessarily suitable for the cities.

How should women's organisations in the urban areas be strengthened?

What sort of training would strengthen effectively their economic role?

How should we fight against violence against women in a cultural context in which talking about yourself or your family is considered shameful for women?

Which strategies would oppose policies which have negative effects on women?

Some answers are already emerging from our experiences with women's organisations. For example, networks of grassroots women's organisations are the soundest base on which to build female solidarity and women's representation. Access to information and training is crucial for women in order to give them more responsibility in the community and in the choices which affect them.

Working with women for sustainable development in countries like Senegal means asking these questions in the context of where women are now, what they have, and what they lack. Access to resources and land is a main issue, as is education and training — particularly for young girls. Reducing domestic workloads, better health care, more information, particularly about family and employment rights so that people know what they are legally entitled to, are all important.

There should be more research on the effects of structural adjustment on women, looking at issues such as children's schooling, remuneration for domestic work, and women's physical and mental health.

The impact of development policies and women's projects should always be studied closely, and this research must take into account the roles the women occupy, the conditions they live in, their status and their relationship with men.

Conclusion

Sustainable development presupposes that, through their active participation, disadvantaged people, of which women rank among the poorest, can determine and control the development process. Therefore, the process should be made more democratic, to accommodate women and recognise their roles.

Demands made by grassroots people themselves, supported by their own organisations, is the indispensable condition for sustainable development. This means creating mechanisms and spaces for women who have something to say. Support for women who are organising themselves can help create and strengthen women's confidence, and thereby boost the whole country's development.

Is it appropriate to work with women without considering their needs, their status, and their roles in society? Is it not rather a case of implementing structural change for a better social system because this will be fairer for the disadvantaged?

Sustainable development also needs fairer relations between the North and the South, built against a background where we recognise each other's characteristics, agree to share 'know-how' and resources.

Development organisations, and all the players in development, have to engage in a new dynamic where each participant will take on his or her own responsibilities in the search for more justice, dignity, and prosperity for the poor sections of society — in particular , for women.

Environment and women in Uganda: the way I see it

Judy Adoko

TONY SWIFT/OXFAM

FROM MY EXPERIENCE in Oxfam, the type of 'environmental' project that exists in Uganda is the type started by an outsider going to a women's group and enlightening the women on the dangers of environmental degradation caused by cutting trees. Women are told that there is drought because trees are being cut for firewood. They are also told that if they do not plant trees, they will have no firewood for cooking. The other benefits put forward for women engaged in such tree-planting projects are income, which they can get from the sale of seedlings, better nutrition for their children from eating fruits and, of course, shade for their homes.

The more advanced environmental projects are involved with improved charcoal-burning stoves which consume less charcoal, thereby saving both charcoal and money; and with composting for fertilising.

Inputs for projects

For women to carry out the tree-planting projects they need, amongst other things, land and water for the seedlings. Traditionally, in most Ugandan cultures, land is used by women but owned by men. There is also a shortage of land; so much so that no group could afford to plant trees on their own, on an empty plot. Most women plant a few trees on either a coffee planta-

tion or banana plantation where the crops are traditionally owned by men. So, whatever good the trees do, they do not directly benefit the women anyway. A woman has to wait for her few trees to mature before she can cut one down to use as firewood. Considering that these trees are only a few in number, how long can she use the firewood for cooking before she has to plant again and wait another two years?

While waiting for the trees to grow, the women continue to water the seedlings, and meet visitors brought to them by NGOs.

In some projects I visited there were signs of seedlings gone to waste because of lack of water; the women had to walk miles to fetch water for their domestic use and just could not keep the seedlings watered. Some schemes have introduced a bicycle which can be used for collecting the water for the seedlings, but this is not available for domestic use. Why, I wonder, does it need a concern for 'environmental issues' rather than women's daily burden of water-carrying before a bicycle is introduced?

Benefits accruing to women

Firewood

The women who plant trees for firewood have to wait two to three years before they can harvest the firewood. Even then the branches are just twigs which could never boil beans. If the trees are planted specifically for firewood, it means that they have to be cut down eventually. How, then, would this contribute to environmental protection? (Perhaps the argument is because they have avoided cutting down another one.)

Environmental Protection

Although I do not have the statistics to show who are the greatest destroyers of trees, I have lived in Uganda long enough to know that in my village firewood is collected from dry trees after the burning of grass in December — not from green trees. After the grass is burnt the women can see more clearly in the bush and pick the dead wood, leaving the green pieces. (As far as I know none of the environmental NGOs in Uganda have touched on grass burning as an environmental issue.) Very, very rarely were green trees cut down for firewood and even then it was only the old women who did this because they were too weak to walk long distances looking for dry trees.

It seems to me that in Uganda the greatest destroyers of trees are the charcoal burners who are business men, sometimes wielding considerable power. If we want a meaningful environmental project, would not they be the best target, rather than the poor village women who already have their arms full of work?

Income

The seedlings are supposed to be sold by the women to raise income. The price for this is usually 50 or 100 shillings per seedling (USH 2,050 to £1). Considering the small amount of money most women have at their disposal, it is no wonder that one woman in a group I visited wanted to start a poultry project for cash. According to her, 'one cannot eat trees'. In one project we found that some seedlings were bought from women's groups by men because it is they who traditionally 'owned' seedlings. They would then grow them and sell them.

Nutrition

Partners involved in environmental projects argue that planting some trees, especially fruit trees, will improve the nutrition level in families. This argument does not hold water with me because most homes I know (in Lango) have planted trees such as mango, orange and (in Buganda) Jack fruit, since long before 'environment' was an issue. I think that this is just a way of trying to impress funders.

In Uganda, the land on which women grow food is owned by men.   JENNY MATTHEWS/OXFAM

Concluding comments

Consider then the following:
- Such environmental tree-planting projects add to women's burden of water collection.

- They do not address gender issues such as ownership of land.
- They do not benefit women immediately either in cash or in firewood.
- They do not benefit the environment for long.
- Women are not the greatest destroyers of trees.
- Fruit has always been available.

Is it fair that women should be burdened with 'environment' which, to me, is a world-wide problem of tomorrow? What can environmental projects also do about the local problems of today?

Cooking over a wood fire, Uganda. The shortage of fuelwood is caused by trees being cut down for profit by charcoal burners. Jenny Matthews/Oxfam

Proposal

It is true that poor people are affected, maybe more than others, by their environment, but I believe that they are already struggling with too many immediate problems to be saddled with 'environment'. This is especially so as they are not the greatest culprits in destroying it.

Therefore, my proposal is that partners should target rich groups to carry out environmental projects, but not women. All that should be done for women is to let them know that environmental degradation is dangerous for them and for their children tomorrow. (As if they did not already know!)

I would further propose that schools, especially primary schools, be used for tree planting in their community. Young boys at home could also be mobilised to grow tree seedlings in their communities. Fetching water and watering the seedlings could become an occupation for the boys, who are relatively free compared to girls.

With regard to the introduction of environmentally improved charcoal-burning stoves: some projects introduce these stoves in villages where charcoal is not used anyway. It is town-dwellers who are the main users of charcoal for cooking and heating. Even so, at current prices improved stoves are too expensive for most people, at 5,000 to 6,000 shillings, compared with 1,200 shillings at the most for ordinary stoves.

Environmental projects should sensitise the charcoal-burning businessmen, if they do not already know of the danger that they are creating. If they do know, we should lobby for laws for sustainable forest management.

Policy statement on population and the environment

In the context of the emerging debate which named population size as a major cause of environmental degradation, three groups — the Social Science Research Council (SSRC), the International Social Science Council (ISSC), and Development Alternatives with Women for a New Era (DAWN) — came together to consider the evidence, each group contributing its own special experience to the exercise. The following statement was formulated at a workshop sponsored by these three groups in Cocoyea, Mexico, in February 1992.

THE CURRENT MACRO-DEBATE which portrays population growth as the central variable in environmental degradation is not supported by research findings. Extremes of wealth and poverty, leading to overconsumption by some and the erosion of livelihoods for others, skewed distribution and use of resources, and patterns of human settlement (including urbanisation) have a stronger demonstrable relationship to environmental degradation than population size *per se*. In addition, macro-global economic strategies and policy decisions are increasingly affecting both people and the natural environment. These findings are supported in study after study.

People have traditionally adapted to and shaped the natural environment through the accumulation of local knowledge and experience. This relationship has been increasingly disrupted as a result of external global forces, notably the globalisation of capital, large-scale technology and communications, subordination within world markets, and rising levels of consumption , particularly in industrialised countries. These processes have eroded livelihoods,

the natural environment. The focus on population growth as the key factor in degrading the environment is thus misplaced.

Because poor women and children are the poorest of the poor, and because of the central role that women play in household and natural resource management, they are particularly affected by the erosion of livelihoods. It has been repeatedly demonstrated that fertility is determined by cultural and socio-economic factors such as women's economic autonomy, legal and political rights, education, health, and access to reproductive health services. Fertility decline is also related to the improved survival chances of offspring. However, general erosion of livelihoods are increasingly undermining women's access to health services (including family planning services) and education.

Policy implications are:

1 Despite current ideologies and policies favouring trade liberalisation free of state regulation, market forces cannot be relied upon to protect the livelihoods of people or the health of the environment.

2 The global community including NGOs

and international institutions, national and local governments have an obligation to protect the environment and to help to ensure the sustainable livelihoods of present and future generations.

3 Extractive industries including mining, logging and petroleum tend to disrupt both the physical and social environment. It is therefore recommended that:

• an international data base of the social, economic and environmental effects of these traded resources be established;

• information drawn from the data base be made available to local communities;

• social and environmental impact studies be commissioned by governments;

• an international code of ethics for extractive companies be incorporated into all concessions and contracts.

4 Intensive agriculture, transformative industries, and military activities, that produce waste and pollution as well as severe social and economic dislocation, adversely affect the environment and the health of people. Critical assessment of the environmental and human effects of these processes is urgently needed.

5 In order to promote the sustainability of agriculture, international organisations, national governments, and producers' associations must develop and disseminate more careful guidelines and regulations, to ensure that the use of modern agricultural technology (fertilisers, pesticides and herbicides, irrigation and machinery) have the least deleterious impact on the environment and people.

6 There must be a reassessment of macroeconomic forces such as debt, resulting structural adjustment programmes, financial and trade flows and agreements, and national government interventions to mitigate their dramatic and damaging effects on the natural environment and livelihoods of the poor.

The focus on population growth as the key factor in degrading the environment is misplaced.

7 In order to promote sustainable development and sustainable livelihoods :

• Management of local resources and the definition of 'environmental problems' must be democratised so that local communities can influence and invoke state regulations and policies which protect their access to resources.

• Women's entitlements and access to key services must increase, for example: education, employment and child care health care for themselves and their families, adequate reproductive health services, equal property and legal rights.

• Women must have a stronger role in decision making.

• People must have increased access to information on the environmental damage of the industrialised products and processes encountered in everyday life.

8 Governments, corporations, academic institutions, and society as a whole must promote more environmentally-sound and sustainable forms of development and technology, including the transfer of environmentally-appropriate technology. To this end, innovative measures must be developed and implemented with respect to national income accounting systems, taxation and legislation.

9 There must be a concerted effort on the part of the local, national, and global communities to change values that have led to overconsumption, so as to promote a new ethic which attaches primacy to caring for people in harmony with the environment.

High-tech hazards: beyond the factory gate

Claire Hodgson and Geraldine Reardon

MICRO-ELECTRONICS is generally considered 'clean technology', the pollution-free answer to the dirty manufacturing processes of the past. The image belies the truth. Micro-electronics manufacturing is dangerous to the health of the workers employed, their families, and the surrounding environment. This is especially the case in countries where workplace and environmental controls are suppressed or non-existent.

Most micro-electornics production takes place in South-East Asia, but manufacturers are always on the look out for more favourable locations. The intense competition in the industry encourages companies to move to regions where incentives are high, wages are low, and environmental controls lax. Eager to attract and maintain investment, local governments in countries as diverse as Mexico, Scotland, Thailand, and the US compete with each other to create company-friendly conditions.

Micro-electronics workers are mostly young women, especially in the demanding work of semi-conductor or 'chip' fabrication and assembly, and companies rely on existing discrimination in local labour markets to keep costs down through low salaries and short-term contracts. Rural women, middle-aged married women, immigrant and ethnic minority women are also recruited, depending on local conditions.

In contrast to the industry's glamorous and ultra-modern image, these women are potentially exposed to a whole array of highly hazardous chemicals and dangerous production processes, very often without adequate health and safety protection.

The manufacture of electronic products uses five major processes, requiring workers to clean, bond, solder, etch and plate, using a wide range of substances such as chlorinated hydrocarbons — suspected of causing cancer — or corrosive acids like hydro-fluoric acid that can cause anything from minor burns to blindness. It is common for chemicals to be heated, a process which can make them even more dangerous, and which widens the area they contaminate.

Common complaints and slack standards

The full and long-term effects of exposure to many of the toxic chemicals used in the industry have yet to be established either by industrial or government-sponsored research. The little that is known — for example, that epoxy resins can cause skin, eye and respiratory problems — should lead to the enforcement of stringent health and safety procedures, but monitoring and enforcement are generally weak.

GTE Lenkurt, a company based in Albuquerque, New Mexico, was taken to court by a former employee dying of cancer. The case uncovered an array of health problems in more than 200 employees — 95 per cent women, 70 per cent Hispanic — including cancers rarely found in New Mexican Hispanics, frequent miscarriages, excessive menstrual bleeding necessitating hysterectomies, and bizarre skin and neurological disorders. Their work was assembling solid-state devices inside electronic components. Management were 'vehemently anti-union, and persistently punitive to workerswho expressed concerns over working conditions'.[1] The company eventually settled out of court — as did the chemical manufacturers Dow, Du Pont, and Shell, charged with distributing dangerous products with insufficient warnings.

There is a widespread lack of knowledge of substances, for example:

By 1980 more than 3,000 new chemicals were being developed annually. Between 700 — 1000 of these substances enter regular commercial use every year.... Of the 45,000 toxic chemicals listed by the US National Institute for Occupational Safety and Health ... 2,500 were identified as carcinogens, 2,700 as mutagens .... Less than 7,000 had been adequately tested.[2]

This worrying lack of research applies to many of the chemicals used in micro-electronics production. Given this, their impact on workers' health and on the environment requires close monitoring by management in co-operation with employees. Yet despite 25 years of production very little data or in-depth case studies are available.

Beyond the factory gates

If women working inside factories are at risk, what is the guarantee that women living outside are not? The hazardous effects of electronics production do not stop at the factory gates.

The industry consumes large quantities of clean air, pure water and highly refined chemical inputs, yet a number of very serious toxic chemical leaks, spills and airborne emissions have been reported over the past 20 years. These reports have been made because there was someone on the look-out; where there are no concerned environmental agencies, governmental or non-governmental, the hazards go undetected. In the US, vigilant community, environmental and labour organisations have worked together to clean up a specific area. In countries where legal safeguards are nil or unenforced, high-tech industrial pollution continues unabated.

Assembling new technology products in Antigua. Most workers in the micro-electronics industry are young women.

PHILIP WOLMUTH/PANOS PICTURES

The Mexico-US border

Along the Mexican side of the Mexico-US border there is an industrial zone called the *maquiladora,* where mainly foreign-owned assembly plants operate. Recently, this zone has begun to expand, largely as a result of the US-Mexico Free Trade Agreement. The *maquiladora* is notorious for its public health and environmental problems. Here, approximately 1,800 mainly US-owned TNCs employ about 400,000 Mexicans (predominantly women) in plants producing automotive and electrical goods, textiles, chemicals, furniture, and ceramics. This has caused widespread environmental concern from such pressure groups as the National Wildlife Federation, the National Toxics Campaign and el Grupo de los Cien. In 1988 researchers at Mexico's El Colegio de la Frontera Norte found that:

> 20 out of 76 maquiladora operations surveyed in the city of Mexicali cited weaker environmental laws in Mexico as a main or important factor for their relocation[3]

Eastman Kodak, US high-tech chemical and electronics manufacturers, ranked in 1988 among the top 20 worst emitters of air-borne toxins in the US in 1988, now operates in Mexico.[4] GTE Lenkurt, the US company mentioned above, has been in Mexico since 1983. Some environmentalists fear that increased competition from the removal of trade barriers will force US industry to cut corners and lower standards. A Mexican Government report points to the same potential danger:

> If it is possible to save money by improperly disposing of dangerous wastes, industry will probably do it ... Industrialists are reluctant to spend their money on proper waste management. The reason could partly me ignorance, but the main motive is probably economic.[5]

In 1990 the total budget of the Mexican environmental agency, SEDUE, was $US3.1 million, comparing dismally to the figure of $US50 million spent annually by the State of Texas to protect air and water. Despite Mexico's recent efforts to tighten up its environmental legislation, and to increase dramatically the budget allocated to SEDUE, environmentalists and labour organisers remain sceptical that these improvements will be effective.

Cleaning up

How do workers, community activists and environmentalists counter the profit motive of an enormous multi-million dollar industry, willing to sacrifice the long-term health of its workers and the environment for short-term financial gain?

Organising for piecemeal improvements is a tactic employed by women in the Signetics Union in Thailand, for example. They successfully established the right of women workers to be tested for chemical levels in the body. Signetics, the employer, now pays for workers with unacceptably high levels to have purifying injections.[6]

Another tactic, used by the Silicon Valley Toxics Coalition, was to lobby for stricter controls and higher penalties for offending companies. The Coalition is an example of united action between worker organisations and community and environmental pressure groups. Where the link between environmental hazards and health and safety in the workplace is clear, stronger local links between labour organisers and environmentalists could strengthen the hand of both parties.

Clinical researchers, such as those at the Research-Action Group at the University of Quebec in Montreal who have carried out extensive work with women employees and ex-employees in the micro-electronics industry, work with union and community participation. Researchers at the Asia Monitor Resource Center in Hong Kong continue to study the situation of women workers in the industry.

In Malaysia, an international conference on health and safety in the micro-electronics industry has been held to look at current research and how occupational health problems in this industry are dealt with in different countries.

If companies organise transnationally, then international collaboration and joint action are also required of researchers, labour and environmental groups. Almost all monitoring and research available on the environmental impact of micro-electronics has been done in industrialised countries. Support for research in the South is necessary, as is making the data already compiled in the North available to women's, labour and environmental groups in the South. This information could be a crucial factor for women organising to improve local conditions, both inside and outside the factory gates.

References

1 Fox, S (1991) *Toxic Work: Women Workers at GTE Lenkurt*, Temple University Press, Philadelphia.

2 Gassert, T (1985) *Health Hazards in Electronics: A Handbook*, Asia Monitor Resource Centre, Hong Kong.

3 Anon (1991) 'Greens Talk Trade', *National Journal*, 13 April.

4 National Wildlife Federation (1991) *Trade and Environment Information Packet*, Washington.

5 ibid.

6 Women Working Worldwide (1991) *Common Interests: Women Organising in Global Electronics*, London.

see also:

Mergler, D et al (1991) 'Visual Dysfunction Among Former Micro-electronics Assembly Workers', *Archives of Environmental Health*, 46: 6.

Huel, G et al (1990) 'Evidence for adverse reproductive outcomes among women microelectronic assembly workers', *British Journal of Industrial Medicine*, 47:400-404.

A bibliography on the subject of women working in micro-electronics is currently being compiled. For further information please write to Women Working Worldwide, Box 92, 190 Upper Street, London N1 1RQ, UK.

Air and water pollution is an increasing problem as Southern countries industrialise. This photograph was taken in India, but smoking chimneys are a health hazard wherever they are.   RAJENDRA SHAW/OXFAM

Finding a voice

Visanthi Arumugam

This article has been drawn from Victims Without Voice: A Study of Women Pesticide Workers in Malaysia, *published in 1992 by Tenaganita, Selangor; and Pesticide Action Network Asia and the Pacific, Penang, Malaysia.*

IN THE PAST women's role in agriculture was grossly underestimated. Although today the role of women in subsistence and small-scale agriculture is more widely recognised, their position in large-scale and plantation farming rarely is. As a result, the health problems they face in this type of agricultural work have been a neglected area of study and action.

'Development' packages, including high-yield varieties of seed, fertilisers, pesticides, irrigation and tractors, have intensified the already acute problems of land scarcity and tenure, and have transformed agricultural methods in order to accommodate the weeding, spraying and transplanting needed for high-yield crops. This form of high-tech, high-input agriculture has been thoroughly criticised by environmentalists for the damage it causes to the soil and water supplies.

On plantations in Malaysia, as elsewhere, women's labour is still used for the most back-breaking and tedious work, all for very little reward — the average earnings of the women who do these jobs are less than men's, and if the seeds are grown on a woman's own family land, the chances are that the woman will have to do all that extra work without pay herself. In addition, women agricultural workers are now faced with the grim fact that their health can be seriously damaged through the unregulated use of pesticides. Pesticide toxicity can also reach unborn children, the damage having been done before the mother realises she is pregnant.

Joint study on Malaysia

In early 1991, Tenaganita[1] and PAN Asia and the Pacific[2] collaborated on a study of the impact of pesticides on women workers on the plantations in Malaysia. This was the first part of a seven-country study on the subject to be undertaken by PAN Asia and the Pacific.

In Malaysia about 40 per cent of the economically-active female population is involved in the agricultural sector. Of the 50,000 field and general workers, 80 to 90 per cent are women. In the plantation sector alone 30,000 women work as pesticide sprayers. Complaints of sore eyes, skin rashes, burnt fingernails, and disruption of menstrual periods are disturbingly common.

In 1988 the Malaysian Minister of Health attributed incidents of pesticide poisoning to unsafe working practices, such as mixing pesticides with bare hands, blowing the nozzle of the sprayer with the mouth to remove blockages, and carrying out spraying operations without regard to basic safety precautions in handling toxic pesticides. He advised estate managers to pay more attention to workers' health, particularly the preventive health aspects. Yet the plantation products of palm oil, rubber and cocoa continue to be a major source of foreign exchange for Malaysia and a major contribution to the fortunes of the owners, while the estate labour force lives in poverty, amid exposure to toxic chemicals.

The study was undertaken to document the extent of the problem in the plantations. It is an attempt to give a voice to the women workers, to record and publicise their plight. Researchers from Tenaganita conducted the survey throughout the months of January to March 1991, living in the community and participating fully in community life, keeping detailed notes on what they heard, saw or felt about the women working with pesticides. A detailed look at the women's socio-economic problems provided a clear understanding of the issues involved. PAN Asia and the Pacific analysed the findings and did the research into the health effects and available legislation on pesticides.

Workshops for women

As part of its Women and Pesticides programme, PAN Asia and the Pacific is organising a series of training workshops during 1991-3, with a special focus on women's groups in Asia. In June 1991 PAN worked closely with Tenaganita in organising the first workshop in Serdang, Malaysia. Twenty participants from ten local organisations attended the five-day event. Two resource persons from Indonesia and a participant from Thailand came to share their experiences and campaign successes in their own countries.

During the workshop, the participants devised strategies for action. Their recommendations were compiled in the *Serdang Declaration*, the first of its kind to address the hazards facing women working in modern agriculture.

1 Tenaganita stands for Kumpulan Tenagapadu Wanita — Action Group of Women Workers — an organisation in Malaysia supporting women workers and carrying out action and research to promote the interests of working women.

2 PAN Asia and the Pacific is a regional centre of the Pesticide Action Network (PAN), a worldwide network which carries out action and research on the hazards associated with pesticides, their causes and their solutions.

Women harvesting cabbages, Malaysia. Growing vegetables commercially requires heavy use of pesticides.

DAVID BULL/OXFAM

The Serdang Declaration

We citizens and representatives of people's organisations from Malaysia, Indonesia and Thailand met to address the issues surrounding pesticide use and abuse, in particular the impact of pesticides on women. We have looked at available alternatives to pesticides and worked out action strategies with clear objectives and recommendations.

The realities

We have been confronted with cases of women suffering from pesticide poisoning including skin damage, nasal bleeding, cracking of fingernails, and problems with the reproductive organs. Over 30,000 women sprayers in Malaysia are daily exposed to pesticides and have very little chance of treatment, cure or even basic first aid. Due to the absence of medical monitoring and the sad state of the health-care system in the plantations, the extent of the impact of pesticides on women, especially on their reproductive health, and the effect on the foetus are unknown. Being women and thus subordinate in the family and community, they continue to suffer silently. Unfortunately, the trade union movement has not effectively taken up their cause, and women workers continue to work in harsh and hazardous conditions.

It is common for women sprayers to use pesticides without the necessary precautions. Many do not use protective clothing when mixing and applying pesticides. The high temperatures and humidity in Malaysia make protective clothing inappropriate and very uncomfortable. The storage and disposal of pesticides is also haphazard. Worse still, the pesticide industry promotes pesticides giving very little information on their dangers.

Similarly, in the farming sector, information on pesticides is merely promotional and persuasive rather than for informed choice. And women farmers share similar problems with their sisters in the plantation sector. Their role as farmers is only recently being recognised and they rarely make decisions on pesticide use on their farms.

At present, there is no comprehensive piece of legislation to protect agricultural workers from unsafe and hazardous working conditions. There are studies to show that the International Code of Conduct on the Distribution and Use of Pesticides (FAO Code) regulations laid down in the Pesticides Act (1974) of Malaysia have been violated.

Vital information

We also recognise that farmers, sprayers, consumers and citizens' groups lack information on and awareness of the hazards of pesticides and their impact on users, especially women, and the environment mainly because:

- There is a lack of reliable information. Independent and continuous research and monitoring of the health of users and of the dangers of using pesticides is lacking.

- The key source of information is from the pesticide industry. When the health and safety data is generated solely by the industry that has a vested interest in the outcome, then misrepresentation becomes possible. In the past, there have been a number of documented cases where such information has been manipulated.

- Information available on health and safety of pesticides and research on hazards is classified confidential. The confidentiality of the information has only helped the pesticide industry, not the users nor the people who are exposed to pesticides directly and indirectly through residues in the food, water and the environment.

As consumers, we are concerned about the lack of information about the levels of residues in our food although we have a laboratory monitoring the situation. In fact, Malaysian consumers came to know there was a problem with pesticide residues only when a neighbouring country rejected our vegetables because of high pesticide residues.

We are also concerned about the use of highly toxic pesticides in the country especially when our farmers and sprayers are not properly trained in their use. Pesticides banned or severely restricted in many countries are still available here. Our country is also involved in producing and exporting pesticides and we are concerned about the health and environmental problems that are caused by their production and use.

Alternatives do work

We are aware that there are viable alternatives to pesticides. There are many successful case studies showing that pesticides are not necessary in the amounts that are being used today. Our reliance on pesticides as the sole method of pest control has led to problems of pest resistance to pesticides and resurgence. These twin problems have caused untold economic hardship to farmers. Farming methods dependent on high capital inputs including pesticides and fertilisers can also accelerate soil erosion and fertility loss, threatening the basis of all agricultural productivity and human sustenance.

As the economic, environmental and social costs of pesticides mount, we believe that we need to change the prevailing methods of food and fibre production if we are adequately to address the problems posed by pesticides. Successful large-scale application of an integrated pest management system has been implemented in Indonesia. Biological control, including conservation of natural predators, has also been demonstrated successfully. We are aware of the growing evidence that sustainable, agro-ecological farming systems offer genuine solutions to the many problems associated with chemical pesticide dependence without sacrificing the yields and efficiencies the world requires.

Networking for change

Concerned with the problems posed by pesticides, citizens' groups have begun linking together both nationally and globally to tackle the problems. One such network is the Pesticide Action Network (PAN). PAN's 'Dirty Dozen' campaign targeted against 12 highly hazardous and widely-used pesticides led to stricter controls on those 12 in some countries. PAN has worked to ensure better implementation of the FAO Code, which provides guidelines on the distribution and use of pesticides, including provision on labelling, advertising, testing and management of pesticides. PAN also provided the information that led to the adoption of the principle of 'prior informed consent'. This principle will help importing nations make informed decisions about hazardous pesticides coming into their country.

We also realise that as long as development and agriculture remains profit-centred with increasing monopoly and control by a few, exploitation of our resources will continue. We need to change that. Our philosophy of development must be people- and environment-centred and we must recognise that we are only custodians of this planet for future generations.

Action agenda

With this concern, vision and philosophy, we make the following recommendations for action:-

1 Recognising that political will and effective control mechanisms are needed, we recommend:

   • the immediate implementation of the Pesticides (Highly Toxic Pesticides) Regulations, 1988;
   • the review of the Pesticides Act so that it is in line with the FAO Code;
   • that the Pesticide Board be moved to the Prime Minister's Department for effective coordination and enforcement;
   • a ban on the use of all highly hazardous pesticides requiring heavy protective clothing since the use of protective clothing is impractical for the hot, humid climate of this country;
   • that paraquat be banned since this pesticide is implicated in a large number of pesticide poisonings and most of the deaths due to pesticides.

2 Recognising that workers in the plantations should be protected from the hazards associated with pesticides andother health problems we call for the enactment of an Occupational Health and Safety Act to cover the plantation industry.

3 Aware that there is a lack of concerted monitoring of the health of those who use and work with pesticides we call upon the Ministry of Health and institutions of higher learning to:

   • conduct research and systematically monitor the short- and long-term impact of pesticide use on the health of workers and citizens;

• to make public all research findings so that workers, farmers and consumers will be able to understand the hazards of pesticides.

4 Knowing the sad state of the health services in the plantation sector we urge the Ministry of Health to ensure that better health-care facilities and basic amenities be provided to workers in the plantation sector.

5 Concerned that consumers are exposed to pesticides through residues in the food, water, and the environment, we call on the Pesticides Board to monitor pesticide residues regularly and to make that information available to citizens.

6 Acknowledging the important role of trade unions in protecting the health and safety of workers, we urge trade unions to:

   • make the pesticide issue into a major labour issue;
   • provide continuous monitoring and education programmes for all sprayers on the dangers posed by pesticides.

7 Aware that women workers and women farmers are being daily poisoned we urge that:

   • all women's groups put the issue on their agenda for action;
   • all citizens' groups begin action and education on pesticide and their impact on health and the environment.

8 Recognising that safer, viable alternatives to pesticides exist we recommend that research into such alternatives be given priority and resources to be made available for their implementation. We urge the Minister of Agriculture to implement a serious Integrated Pest Management (IPM) policy that would minimise the use of pesticides.

The challenge

Minimising and curbing pesticide use and creating the climate for the implementation of agro-ecological systems of food and fibre production on a wide scale will, no doubt, present a great challenge. It is a challenge we, as individuals and groups, have accepted with our own agenda for action. We are committed to realising the goals for a sustainable and people-centred development through our action to curb pesticide misuse and overuse. We commit ourselves to working closely with workers in the plantations, farmers including those involved in the FELDA and FELCRA schemes, and with consumers.

Our action for change will be developed through a comprehensive and holistic strategy of research and information gathering, education and consciousness raising, organising and mobilising, advocating legal reforms and through legal action, and promoting the development of alternatives including sustainable agriculture.

In order to realise our goals and vision at the national and global levels, we hope to consolidate and strengthen our actions through a pesticide action network in the country. We urge other groups and concerned individuals to join us.

Women in environmental disasters: the 1991 cyclone in Bangladesh

Rasheda Begum

In the late evening of 29 April 1991, a cyclone hit the eastern coast of the Bay of Bengal. Winds of 225kph and tidal surges up to six metres swept across heavily populated off-shore island and coastal communities. The force of the storm was concentrated between Chittagong to the north and Cox's Bazar to the south. Casualty rates and destruction were catastrophic. The full extent of human fatality and economic loss will never be known, but over 100,000 lives were lost.

I finished my cyclone relief work at Bashkali on 23 May. During the 23 days I spent there I saw the death toll of women become the commodity used to attract the sympathy of the relief donors. The real needs of the women in the wake of this disaster, however, were ignored by the Government and by the relief agencies.

I found that women had died in greater numbers than men, not just because they were physically weaker, but because of Bangladesh's male-dominated social structure, underpinned by religious traditions, which restricts the mobility of women. Social norms and cultural restrictions confine women to the *protection* of men. Women are not considered an equal partner in marriage, yet they are expected to fulfil certain essential roles, especially to take physical responsibility for the children. During the cyclone women died risking their lives to save their children. The second main responsibility is to guard the family property, including house and livestock. When asked if she had heard the cyclone warning in time to reach safety, one survivor said yes, but that she did not leave for fear of being blamed and punished if anything should happen to the property in her absence.

Although disaster is a general concern which affects both women and men, it is particularly a women's concern when the social rules which govern their movements limit their access to relief supplies and safety; and when their gender is used to obtain relief — food and other assistance — which is then not fairly distributed. In desperation people can become unruly and aggressive, and it is women who often lose in the battle.

As a woman relief worker, I learned specific lessons from these experiences. First of all, the events surrounding this cyclone have shown that in environmental disasters women are made more vulnerable by their social status, both during and after the full impact of the event; and secondly, while it is necessary to have more women involved in relief work, discrimination can seriously impede their work.

My experience of food distribution

Two colleagues and I reached Chittagong on 1 May, three days after the cyclone. Little information was available, but we decided to work at Bashkhali Upazilla, believing this to be the worst-hit area. It was not until later that we learned that the whole coastal area had been equally devastated. We spent the whole of the next day trying to procure food.

Chittagong itself had been badly affected so supplies were scarce and prices high. At last we managed to hire a truck and buy some *mori* (puffed rice), molasses, bananas, biscuits, candles and matches.

On the way to Bashkhali the effects of the tidal waves, cyclonic wind, and rain could be seen. Most of the trees were burnt or uprooted and electricity poles were down. The smell of dead bodies — of animals and people — hung in the air.

In Bashkhali the market had suffered damage and there was no food to eat. Oxfam was the first NGO to arrive with food supplies. We joined a meeting of government officials, army officers, political leaders, and some of the local elite, who were discussing the burial of the hundreds of bodies — already 400 had been buried. In the meeting we jointly decided to go to Chonua, one of the Union of Bashkhali.

The next day we started for Chonua. Sixty people were carrying our goods from the truck to an embankment where thousands of people were waiting for food when one of the workers, overcome by weakness, dropped a packet of biscuits. Suddenly scores of men, women and children rushed for the biscuits. It was then we realised just how desperate for food they were, so we sent for extra supplies and decided to work with the help of local volunteers.

I walked more than two miles to

High tide at Shurjodia village, after the 1991 cyclone in Bangladesh.   Shahidul Alam/Oxfam

Chonua. Along the cold, muddy, slippery road I came across thousands of bodies of women, men and children, as well as goats, cows and chickens. Houses were demolished and trees uprooted. People showed us the bodies of women lying flat on their back. They told us this was done by immoral people to get at the women's ornaments, explaining that women's dead bodies are normally placed face down.

At Chonua we crossed a canal to reach the embankment where people were waiting for food. We saw people who, in their misery, could no longer even cry for the loss of their near and dear ones. A few, with outstretched hands, were crying from hunger.

At this stage it seemed nearly impossible to distribute things systematically. I formed a committee of students, local government people and one government relief worker. In the meantime the people had become more distraught and impatient. I guessed that some were planning to snatch the food from us.

With the help of the military, I took half the food off the boat. When distribution started the people could not be kept organised. They were all rushing to get food, some hitting and biting the volunteers, others taking twice their share. All the disturbance was created by men; women were pushed down and left behind in the rush. I ordered the distribution to stop and sought help from the women. One of the women stood up with a bamboo stick and told them not to be so undisciplined or the food might be taken away. The tactic worked: two long lines were made for women, men were not allowed to join them, and half the food was distributed quickly.

In the meantime, however, a local MP had intervened and ordered government supplies of rice to be given to the women in one of the lines. When this started the men joined the line and chaos broke out again. Taking the opportunity, some of the people snatched packets of biscuits and molasses which I had reserved for women. As they ran away, others pushed them over, grabbed the goods and fled. By this time I was tired and felt I had lost the strength and mental courage to continue. I took the advice of local people, including the women who had helped in the distribution, and left the supplies in the hands of a trusted person in the village, so that I could return to organise the rest of the distribution programme. After walking the two miles back I stayed the night with the family of an Upazilla judge, as the guest house was full of higher government officials who had come to monitor the relief work.

Distribution on subsequent days

The next day I received another truck load of pressed rice and molasses from Oxfam. I sought help from the local administration but they said they were too busy with the government relief programme and with attending to the visiting government officials. They asked me to hand over our goods to them as they had a shortage, and as a woman alone I would be unable to handle it.

Instead I formed a team of volunteers made up of students and teachers from an NGO called UTTARAN, and informed the police and the UN of our decision to go to Khankhanabad, where relief had not yet reached, and said I would inform them if any problems arose. They tried to stop me leaving, on the grounds that it was not safe for women there — despite the fact that I was with a group of volunteers. The volunteers supported and encouraged me but the UN representative angrily said he would not accept responsibility for the risk I was taking. I reminded him that he had no authority over me and that he could not insist that I do what he wished.

Again, when I requested storage space for our relief goods he said I had to have permission from the magistrate — something I had not heard before. Eventually I got space for one night only. I realised that they were creating difficulties in order to make me hand over the supplies to them.

When we got to Mosherp Alis Bazar it was hard to pass through without responding to the cries and pleas for food, so we decided to start our distribution from there. I instructed the people to make two lines, one for women and one for men. We gave them enough food for one day and moved on, but not before being asked for other necessities. One old woman asked me whether we had any cloth to give some young girls who were not in a position to come out to take the relief food. Another wanted to know if a woman doctor was available. She had had a miscarriage and was suffering pain. Another woman told how she had lost her infant and her breast had become puffy and she felt feverish. I could do nothing for them.

From there we went by boat to East Dongra. Dead bodies were lying scattered and floating everywhere. On seeing me, a number of women ran through the water to the distribution point to tell me of their experiences. Because I, a woman, was there others, too, dared to come out. Most had lost at least some of their children and their husband and many had serious injuries. They asked for medicines, and clothes to keep their children warm. Some were asking for ORS as diarrhoea had started in the area. I saw one woman who had been hit in the pelvic area and could not sit down. The men organising the relief line were telling everyone to sit down and she did not want to tell them why she could not.

Everyone was very distressed. I asked them if they had heard the warning of the cyclone. Some had, but as they had heard it so many times before, with no cyclone occurring, they did not believe it. One

Women's responsibility for home and children makes them particularly vulnerable at times of environmental disaster. Post–cyclone, Bangladesh, 1991.   Shahidul Alam/Oxfam

woman said she heard it but was afraid that she would be blamed and punished if anything happened to the family property in her absence. Others told of similar fears, of not daring to leave the house without their husband's permission.

The team returned to Upazilla and discussed the problem of how to cover a greater area and how to distribute supplies separately for women. We met the medical team, which included two women doctors, described the injuries and illnesses we had seen and explained how women would not show their injuries to a man. They could not leave their post so they asked us to tell people to come to them, although many of the people we had seen were incapable of walking that far.

On 6 May, in a conservative area in Pakuria Union, we again distributed the food in two separate lines as women were not coming to the distribution line because they did not think they could stand side by side with men. Although shelters with kitchens had been set up in schools and temples, many people were leaving them because they feared for the safety of their daughters.

Experience of an earlier cyclone saved many lives. When this cyclone started many people climbed coconut trees which had been planted on an embankment following a previous cyclone. After the cyclone, when all the water was polluted, people survived for three days on the juice and flesh of the coconuts.

Working with other agencies we continued to distribute food in the area using a card system. Although I had distributed the cards in women's names, many were brought by men. I can only assume that child care, illness, or conservativism kept women away from the relief posts.

Finally on 23 May UTTARAN arranged a concluding meeting. I thanked all who had assisted and gave a report of our work over the past 20 days and my assessment of the current situation facing the survivors. I asked for the special health issues of women and the needs of women with children to be fully considered in the relief and rehabilitation programme. The UN officer thanked me and said that he had not believed that a woman could do so much.

Lessons learned as a woman relief worker

In an environmental disaster where people as a whole are vulnerable, poor people are more vulnerable; and it is women who bear the burden of managing the survival of the household under crisis. If more women than men died as a result of the cyclone it is not only because of their physical weakness, but also because they were unable to use their decision-making powers and their physical strength; and they were more involved in saving their children's lives.

Development work should be started straight after the relief and rehabilitation programme. In the case of Bangladesh, research has shown that children in this coastal belt are now dangerously malnourished. If this is so, their mothers must also be malnourished.

In addition to the problems I have mentioned above, there are others I faced and from which I can draw recommendations for future relief work.

Volunteers

There should be more female volunteers. In the case of a major disaster, male volunteers can not adequately meet women's needs. In a disaster people generally find women more approachable than men, yet most relief workers are men.

Women relief workers face higher security risks and obstructiveness from local male leaders and government officials when trying to carry out their work. More women volunteers should be available to form a strong group, able to overcome these problems collectively.

Female doctors and nurses should be included in the volunteer team, alongside a male medical team. Emergency medicine and equipment should be available to cope with women's special needs. For example, many women lose their breast-feeding infants in environmental disasters. Pumps to express breast milk must be available, in order to avoid serious infection and debilitating pain. Equipment and medication is needed to handle the inevitable miscarriages. None of this equipment can be dispensed, or care can be given by men.

Poor women, especially, know fewer languages so local volunteers are needed to overcome language problems, in order to get access to the women more easily and to understand their specific needs.

In addition, all volunteers should be prepared for a different diet, sanitation facilities, and language. They should be aware of the conservative nature of Bangladesh society, and its habits and customs.

Distribution

Women are not only victims themselves but their needs are linked with those of their children. To address women's needs adequately they should be considered both as victims and as having the additional responsibility for children.They should get first priority, and a separate distribution line needs to be organised for them.

This is most important for pregnant and breast-feeding mothers. In particularly conservative areas women may need house-to-house distribution. Without it, women have great difficulty, for practical and social reasons, to come to the distribution line to compete in the struggle for food supplies, elbowing and pushing, with men.

Clothing is an essential part of emergency relief. Protection against the cold is necessary for everyone, but more so for children. A disaster does not make women immune from public censure. They must be fully clothed go out to get food.

Information and management of relief operations

When the relief team reaches the area, they need to get adequate information and to set up a management plan for relief distribution and for the implementation of rehabilitation programmes. Inform-ation from local people, including women, should be obtained, as well as government information. Longer-term relief must be co-ordinated locally. Local volunteers will be needed to deal with different stages of a disaster and to carry out relief work effectively. Local women are more reliable informants as they are less prone to corruption. Students and teachers may also have a role.

Selection of relief goods

After finishing the first phase 'dry and cooked food distribution', a survey should be carried out to collect statistics on how many people are in need, what cooking materials they have, and what fuel is available, before starting the second phase of distribution of uncooked food like rice and pulses. Local food habits may also be considered at this stage. This can be a significant factor in a 'feeding programme'. For example, during the cyclone relief people were given nutritious yet unfamiliar food. They did not know how to cook it and as a result could not eat it. The supplies were wasted and the people were still hungry.

Co-ordination

Proper co-ordination among the different relief teams and with the government relief efforts should be maintained. In the short term, overlap of relief programmes must be avoided to ensure all opportunities are open to everyone. For the longer term they must develop arrangements for strategic planning.

Enduring the drought: the responses of Zambian women

1 Background to the drought

Robin Palmer

SOUTHERN AFRICA ENJOYS only one rainy season, from October or November to March or April. Almost no rain falls outside that period. Consequently if the rains are bad — and they are notoriously fickle and unreliable — consequences can be very serious. Hence agriculture, both 'modern' and 'traditional', is and always has been an extremely hazardous occupation in Southern Africa. Droughts are regular phenomena, but they tend to be localised and limited in scope. This year is different.

The current drought in the Southern African region as a whole is the worst for 50 years in terms of its extent and scale. After a promising start at the beginning of the rainy season, which saw many crops growing well, in January and February (when it should rain almost every day) virtually no rain fell in many parts of the region. This was coupled with extremely high temperatures, so that growing crops simply withered. (In some parts, however, there had been no rain at all earlier in the season, so people were unable to plant anything.)

Many Southern Africans live in urban areas but the bulk of the population still remains dependent on rainfed agriculture. Because of a long history of labour migration, in some countries most rural people are women and children. Some areas are accustomed to droughts. Others, such as the Eastern Province of Zambia, are not. Here, people with limited or no drought experience will find it difficult to cope.

The effects of the drought are compounded by the fact that the countries which normally produce a surplus for export to the rest of the region in years of shortage, notably Zimbabwe and South Africa, will this year have no surplus and will themselves be importing. Conse-quently, yellow maize and other cereals will have to be imported on a huge scale (approximately 11 million tons), principally from the USA and South America. This will inevitably place huge strains on the ports, railways and main road routes in the region. There are also likely to be major problems of distribution at the district level, especially in countries like Zambia, where the infrastructure has crumbled in recent years.

It is important to stress that Southern Africa is not like the Horn of Africa. Though drought has always posed a threat to its people, it is not a region characterised by a dependency syndrome, nor is it one where people have left the land in vast numbers and flocked into urban areas or feeding centres, as has happened in recent years in the Horn. (The partial exceptions are Angola and Mozambique, but movements there have been caused by war rather than by drought.)

The reason for this is because Southern Africans have developed all kinds of 'coping strategies'. In precolonial times these included complex grain-storage systems, hunting, trading, mining, livestock use, foraging and barter. A wide variety of crops were grown to spread risks and as insurance against drought. Under colonial rule, these were supplemented but sometimes replaced or undermined by alternatives linked to the cash economy — by wage labour, piece work, or relying on help from employed urban relatives. Traditional storage systems fell into decay as people grew accustomed to trading surpluses for cash. A narrower range of crops was grown, with an overwhelming tendency to concentrate on maize, for both consumption and sale, because maize was the staple food of migrant workers. Land alienation and population growth reduced per capita grain production. Food distribution became less egalitarian, and rich and poor no longer fasted or feasted together. Food was regularly available to those who could afford it, and scarce for those who could not. The sexual division of labour also changed. For the first time crops became a source of individual gain, rather than nourishment for the whole family. Women's productivity decreased, but their workloads increased. In recent years, as opportunities for wage labour have diminished, this escape route in times of drought has narrowed.

From 20 April to 20 May 1992, Oxfam staff made an intensive tour of the drought-stricken areas of the Eastern Province, holding community-based workshops. The Province is one of Zambia's traditional bread baskets, normally exporting maize and other crops.

These workshops were intended to assess the situation; to identify the most pressing problems and activities communities could undertake to help themselves; to work out operational strategies and community work programmes; and to support local sustaining capacities. Multi-sectoral meetings were held with top district officials to pass on knowledge from the workshops. The following accounts of women's responses to the drought are based on Nawina Hamaundu's detailed reports on the drought in the Eastern Province.

2 Women in the Eastern Province: more hit by drought and yet more enduring

Nawina Hamaundu

HUNDREDS OF WOMEN attended our four workshops in the worst hit areas of Petauke and Nyimba: Luembe, Nyalugwe, Kalindawalo and Mwape. The women who came were able to participate fully in all discussions and finally got a place in their village leadership, thanks to their great determination.

Women in all the areas we visited hold their families together by providing for almost all family needs. They walk for two to three hours in search of water. In villages with open wells, they sometimes do not have the tins and ropes to get the water out of the wells, which means a further walk of about an hour to borrow a rope and tin, draw water then return the rope.

In the worst-hit drought areas of Petauke and Nyimba, women give up their share of food to members of their families. In one village 87 women have lost their husbands because of the drought. These men have not died, they have gone off to marry in other villages where food is available. Some have left behind several children.

Women have, in reality and without recognition, been the main providers for their households

Women are overworked and their problems have been increased by the drought. Women have to walk very long distances in search of water — on average 3-4 hours a day. In addition, women fetch firewood. But they need less wood, as they have almost nothing to cook, except wild roots, depending largely on wild fruits eaten raw. Food is scarce and people, especially old women, are starving. They are very thin and suffer badly from diseases such as dysentery, diarrhoea and scabies, skipping meals in order to feed their children. Women identified pregnant and lactating mothers as the most vulnerable. Nutrition status is poor especially in young children and old women, who are very thin, very fragile. Of the 32 reported dead 18 were women.

Women have no high-value assets, such as cows and land; but some have chickens and goats, although there are few of these left. Their cash income, mainly from subsistence farming and beer brewing, has come to an end with the almost nil harvest. Except for the very few who belong to a women's club, women had no access to credit facilities last season. Women sing a lot of love and sex-related songs, maybe because there are so few men. The source of income is mainly subsistence farming. Land is owned by their husbands or brothers and uncles. One out of a hundred women owned their own *lima* (1 acre plot). Decisions are generally made by men, although women are consulted.

Although village women have been widely neglected it is amazing how, with a little encouragement, they were able to stand up and be fully involved in all decisions in their communities. Our stay and our workshops in Petauke and Nyimba were of immense learning and sharing — an experience which we found highly stimulating and gratifying, especially so because by the end of all our workshops we got the commitment of the men, notably the Chiefs, fully to support the women.

We were given some fascinating glimpses into the lives of really strong women. Women like Tendani Bandawa who, with six children and a husband who had just run away, could stand up in a crowd of over one thousand people and announce that she would like to be fully involved in her village's development. Tandani stood up, her head held up with pride and no self-pity. Our rural sisters are amazing; I wonder how we, their town sisters, would have reacted under such circumstances. Somehow, I think we would have been heart-broken and depressed.

Both at village and district level, I am confident that women will help everyone break through the drought tragedies. The drought will give women the chance to improve themselves and their communities. It is so severe that there has been a breakdown in the traditional male-dominated social structures and now women have to take over. Women have, in reality and without recognition, been the main providers for their households and communities. Our workshops have succeeded in affirming women's vital roles and helping society recognise their immeasurable inputs.

In spite of hunger and psychological pressure, women continue to be loving and cheerful. They were able to sing and dance in appreciation of our visits. We were very touched and we will endeavour to give these new leaders our full support.

Petauke District — Chief Kalindawalo's area

There is generally a widespread scarcity of food in the village's households. Women have to wake up as early as 4:00am to travel at least 10 kilometres to neighbouring villages in search of water from deeper wells. Even then, most of the areas with deep wells lack ropes and buckets for drawing water. In some areas where boreholes had been sunk, these are either dry or are in a state of disuse, needing repair.

The workshop was attended by people from six areas representing 195 villages. These villages have approximately 3,000 to 6,000 people in each. We had 2,981 people at the meeting: 963 women, 2018 men.

In Mwape many families have not had a meal in weeks. They depend on roots, wild fruit and even dead game meat. The old, especially women, have not been leaving their huts due to weakness caused by hunger. They lay in their huts, waiting for death. The poorest in this area have, in desperation, resorted to eating wild roots, which are poisonous if eaten raw. It is first soaked in water for three days to extract the poison and then boiled for one whole day before being eaten. This root is known to have claimed the lives of a number of children, old people, and widows.

There are many children, and almost no child spacing. Many children die young, so women continue giving birth hoping to have at least a few survive.

Women depend on their husband's land, so single women have small portions, while many have none. In rainy years they do *ganyu*; that is, work as cheap labourers for the better-off. Their nutritional status is generally very poor, especially in the elderly, children and breast-feeding mothers who are pathetically thin with long hanging breasts at which their thin and crying babies keep pulling. Families want to support each other but, due to the intense hunger and poverty, sharing and supporting is quickly fading away.

Nyimba District

The drought is in its third year and at its worst, having affected a population of 52,000. Wells, boreholes and dams have gone dry and domestic livestock are nearly extinct. People in this area were reportedly on the verge of starvation. They have begun to eat the same poisonous root as in Petauke District. Some people eat only once in three days. Six deaths from hunger, were reported in three villages. Another cause of death, particularly in children and the aged, was dysentery. Those reported to be suffering most were widows, orphans, the disabled and the aged.

In Luembe 690 people attended the workshop, 410 men, 280 women. It was a touching experience to shake the frail bony hands, especially of the old women. In Nyalugwe, the people were less welcoming.

Women in Zambia's Eastern Province prepare land for planting when and if the rains come. Oxfam's Food for Work programme is also helping local people deepen their well.　Judy Raven/Oxfam

From time immemorial women in Zambia have been overloaded with work and emotional and mental burdens.

Here there were noticeably more women than men; it was later we found out that several men had left their wives to go where there was food. The men looked frustrated, hungry and angry — exhausted. Speaking about hunger, one old man stood up and shouted, 'The Government has lost this year. A very big loss indeed, it has lost because men are not strong enough to produce babies, due to our hunger!' (Possibly a relief for women?)

Six months ago women formed a club to try to address their hunger problems. But due to the hazardous road to Nyimba most of their plans of buying and reselling have not been successful.

In both Luembe area and at the multi-sectoral meeting it was satisfying to have almost half the committee members women. Women in these villages are amazingly humble. In spite of their poverty and the excessive workload, they usually feed their husbands and children first.

Power through participation

The women in the Eastern Province do not have enough rights and freedoms to enable them to assert their dignity and worth as human beings. They are often treated as second-class citizens, both at grassroots level and BOMA (district government) level.

The drought may open new horizons for women because in the tense hunger situation more and more men are turning to women for help. Women's needs can be met without high-cost inputs. They need clean water, improved health, access to basic education, control over child bearing and access to small amounts of credit to help them explore their potential and enable them to feed their families.

We visited six districts in Eastern Province and 12 chiefdoms. In all these areas the drought has brought major changes to overworked rural women. From time immemorial women in Zambia have been overloaded with work and emotional and mental burdens. The Eastern Province is renowned for having more women than men and yet it has been dominated by a few men. For years women have been subjected to various forms of oppression, especially lack of access to decision making. For example, men could marry off daughters at an early age without consulting their mother or other women in the family.

The number of girl children enrolled in schools is almost a third of the number of boys and yet all the areas we visited have more girl children. Most women are illiterate; some have attended primary school. For most girls in the Eastern Province they grow from babyhood directly to womanhood. Girls at the age of 12 are mothers and wives.

Women who had been supported through a club or church are much better off than the rest of the communities. Oxfam-supported women's groups have enough food to last them to about August (1992). They are determined to work hard to help solve some of their numerous problems. In particular women need water and food urgently for themselves and their families.

Our workshops brought a lot of hope to women and encouraged them to work and support each other. We encouraged the full participation of women and we were pleased with their responses. They were able to express themselves in their own language and finally got themselves into the decision-making committees that will try to tackle problems caused by the drought.

After the fisheries: the story of Sinalhan

Eugenia Pina-Lopez

Adapted from Gender needs assessment in the fisheries sector, *report prepared for Oxfam by WRRC. This case study is based on a participatory research project undertaken by a task force: Oxfam UK, WRRC, PACAF, Shield, and CERD.*

The quiet death of Laguna Lake

The Laguna de Bay area covers 90,000 hectares around Laguna Lake in Southern Tagalog, south-east of Manila in the Philippines. The decline of fish production began in the mid-1960s, first as a result of industrial pollution, and then from the commercial practice of mechanical snail gathering. Mechanically scraping snails from the lake bottom has two damaging effects on the adult fish population: 'fingerlings' (young fish) are taken as an unintentional by-catch of the snail gathering, and fish breeding grounds are destroyed.

In the late 1970s the situation deteriorated further following the construction of the first commercial fishpens. The high financial returns generated by this form of aquaculture led to uncontrolled expansion of fishpens along the shallow coastline of the lake, destroying completely the traditional small-scale fisheries. Now the area is part of a massive government- and foreign-financed regional development plan.

Sinalhan is a community — a long narrow strip, part urban, part rural, along the lake — in the Laguna de Bay area. Along the road running through Sinalhan are shops, and small stalls selling cooked food, tended by women also looking after small children. The dwelling units are separated from each other in an orderly geometric pattern by narrow paths. Flowers and plants brighten up what would otherwise be a drab arrangement of small and medium-sized unpainted buildings made of bamboo and cement. At the back of some houses are patches of vegetable gardens, also tended by women. A few metres beyond the gardens, is a large, quiet, almost dead, lake. No boats or fisherfolk can be seen on or off the shore. Compared to the hustle and bustle of the roadside, the lakeside is a picture of barrenness and decay.

It is generally assumed that fishermen are the first, or the only, ones to suffer when they have to stop fishing. This is rarely the case; women in fishing communities are as economically tied to the resource as are their men. They are also vulnerable to the psychological effects of loss of income and social status, having once been independent business women selling and processing fish, and providing investment finance for fishing gear.

I visited Sinalhan in 1990 with representatives of the NGO task force and learned of the slow but steady death of Laguna Lake and the drastic changes this has brought to the lives of the villagers deprived of their traditional livelihoods. The following account of this visit shows how environmental degradation, caused by outside intervention, affects the whole community and how women find ways to cope with reduced status and income.

From prosperity to poverty

Women look back to the 1970s as a prosperous period for their village. Then the lake yielded an abundant supply of good-quality fish, enabling many to have a relatively comfortable life in which needs were adequately met and part of the family income was saved. Many also remember their full-time work in fish marketing and processing and compare it with the harder and less rewarding work they do now.

Between the late 1970s and the early 1980s, the deterioration of the lake occurred steadily and rapidly. The amount and quality of fish steadily dwindled and within ten years the lake has reached a stage of decay and death. The incomes of the small fisherfolk have been diminished and new sources of income had to be found.

What caused the lake to die and why was nothing done about it? The fisherwomen and their husbands identify two major factors: firstly, the pollution caused by waste emptied into the lake from the factories that have mushroomed in the last two decades as the government launched its ill-conceived and unregulated industrialisation programme for Southern Tagalog; and secondly, the unscrupulous construction and expansion of private fishpens, most of which are owned by military men and politicians close to the centres of power. Large areas of the shoreline, now covered with commercially valuable fishpens, came under armed guard. In effect, these aquaculture developments 'privatised' access to inshore waters — the traditional fishing grounds of the fishing communities. The fishermen were pushed farther and farther into the lake until their non-motorised *bancas* (small boats/rafts) could go no further.

By the time the Government began to look at the problems of Laguna Lake, it was already preoccupied with its plan to tap and develop cheap water sources for Metro Manila; and to speed up implementation of

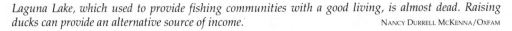

Laguna Lake, which used to provide fishing communities with a good living, is almost dead. Raising ducks can provide an alternative source of income.   NANCY DURRELL MCKENNA/OXFAM

Calabarzon, a massive development plan for the region featuring new industrial, tourist and residential sites. The resulting closure of the Napindan Channel has contributed directly to the lake's deterioration.

The lake has been brought to near death by various (and frequently overlapping) commercial and government interests. The fishing communities, which for centuries have lived beside it, have been left out of this mad scramble for Laguna Lake. As a consequence their lives have been ruined and their future made bleak and uncertain.

One woman showed members of the team a part of her house which was once a thriving store but which she had to close down because of the inability of the fisher families to pay their mounting debts.

The process of reconstruction and strategies for coping

Fishermen rarely go out into the lake any more. Those who persist almost always come back empty-handed. A few bring home small quantities of *agungin* and *biya* — small fish for drying. Although those the team spoke with admit that their earnings are grossly inadequate they continue to fish because it is the thing they know how to do best.

The fishermen see their immediate economic problems as being brought about by a lack of sophisticated fishing gear; the competition for resources with fishpen operators and large-scale fishing boats; a lack of capital; and the high prices of daily goods. They see all of these factors aggravated by the Government's development projects.

Since leaving the fishery, employment for most men has been erratic. An interview with a group of Laguna women, focusing on economic activities, revealed that their husbands have moved from one temporary job to another, usually as construction workers and tricycle (local transport) drivers.

Women in both the urban and rural fish-

The fishing communities, which for centuries have lived beside it, have been left out of this mad scramble for Laguna Lake.

ing communities have taken on a more important role in the household's finances. To enable their families to survive, the women, who once had a relatively relaxed time working in fish marketing, now find themselves taking up more physically strenuous service work. Laundering has emerged as the major occupation and a principal source of income. The reliance on women's income is partly a result of the steady and regular nature of the jobs they find, unlike male employment in construction and transport. Laundering, is an essential household function with a stable demand. As it is not part of the formal sector women can negotiate their terms more easily, especially as their customers are usually better-off relatives and friends living in nearby communities. The pay is, however, low and compares unfavourably with their previous income from fish processing and marketing.

Many women also grow and sell vegetables. Twice a week they harvest a few items for sale in the community. This makes a substantial contribution to an overall low weekly household income. Others raise small animals such as chickens, ducks and pigs. This is, however, an occupation only available to those who can afford to invest in the stock; most are prohibited by a lack of capital. The acquisition of credit by the women is a major focus of survival in the area. Tending *sari-sari* stores (small neighbourhood shops) and cooked-food stalls are other sources of cash income for women. For family consumption, women and children gather snails by the lakeside.

Although the women and their husbands have become heavily dependent on non-fishing activities, high in the women's consciousness is their continued identification as fisherfolk. There remains much hope that their households will someday return to fish catching and marketing. They regard laundering as a necessary yet temporary measure. Everyone spoke of how back-breaking the work is, particularly when compared to fish-vending work. It appears, too, that laundering has a negative impact on their self-esteem. The team sensed a feeling of sadness, embarrassment and also resentment in many of those who admitted that they are now laundry women.

The rural community in Sinalhan has been able to maintain clean and well-kept surroundings, in spite of the absence of adequate public facilities and social services. However, water is a community-wide problem. Women need to fetch water from several pumps, a task that is both labour-intensive and time-consuming. In order to optimise their efforts they have resorted to bathing their small children and washing clothes near the pump. This group activity gives the women an opportunity to chat with one another, thereby turning an ordinary task into a more enjoyable event. They also discuss more worrying matters, one of which is the serious threat of contamination from the water. The pumps draw ground water polluted by a mixture of dumped waste material, one of the causes of the decline in the fishery.

Public-sector health services are inadequate throughout the Philippines. Although there is a community health centre in Sinalhan, there are rarely qualified staff in attendance. Women tend to deal with family illnesses by self-medication, often with herbal medicine. This, however, applies only to simple ailments, such as coughs, cold or fever. In interviews women expressed their preference for their children to be taken care of by a private doctor which, most often, they are unable to afford. Private health care is resorted to only in cases of very serious illnesses.

The twin factors of insufficient income and inadequate health services are forcing women to disregard their own reproductive health care. One woman, already seven months into her fifth pregnancy, has never had any prenatal examination, except once during her first pregnancy. She says that lack of money prevents her from consulting a doctor. She is hoping that the midwife will visit the community health centre soon, so that she can have a free check-up. Another woman complained of a long-standing skin allergy and suspects that she is anaemic but is helpless to do anything about these problems, again because of lack of money.

According to the women met by the team, their life would have been more difficult without the help of relatives. Assistance through this extended family network ranges across material, social and moral dimensions. Women who do laundry rely on women relatives to look after their small children, and better-off relatives provide them with regular, laundry work. A kinship system linking families with one another may be a critical factor in cushioning the impact of the people's current dislocation, and women play a dynamic role in activating and sustaining such exchanges of support.

Organising for the future

SHIELD is an NGO formed in 1989 to assist dislocated fisherfolk families in the Southern Tagalog region. One of its first projects was to set up an all-male organisation to deal with the concerns of fishermen. In early 1990, in response to the rising consciousness of SHIELD women staff of the need to promote the rights and welfare of women in development work, SHIELD set up a separate organisation, NKLS, Naglalaisang Lakas ng Kababaihan (United Women Power).

By then several women in the community were already aware of the potency of unified community action and were actively supporting their husband's organising work. The women tell how they would prepare food for the meetings and listen to the discussions, without being able to participate.

SHIELD's organising activities are currently focused on addressing the community's immediate survival needs, combined with an education programme to explain the structural roots of the community's problems. Throughout, it promotes the ideals of gender equality and people-powered progress.

In explaining why they joined, the members of NKLS say it is a way of responding to their family's poverty. In particular, they express much enthusiasm for the prospect of forming a women's credit co-operative that would provide members with soft loans for economic livelihood projects, such as livestock raising, *sari-sari* stores, or home-based sewing. For them, whatever

their family gains out of the work of the organisation is their personal gain as well. In this area, rural women's identification of 'self' is as part of the social unit, the family, rather than as a personal entity.

Not all women are able to participate in NKLS. They cite their traditional household functions and their recently intensified economic activities as the main barriers. One woman spoke of how her husband refused to let go to the meetings because 'no one would be left to take care of the small children'. Another says that there is simply not enough time or energy left after washing clothes all day.

Women speak of the physical strain and mental stress they have experienced since the closure of the fishery. For some, community activism is just one more job that needs doing. It remains with those women who do have enough time and energy to be active, to build up the organisation for the future benefit of their sisters.

Determined to enable their families to survive, women in Sinalhan have taken up laundry-work to earn a little money.   NANCY DURRELL MCKENNA/OXFAM

Looking for a regenerative approach to sustainability

Nanneke Redclift

This is an edited version of a paper written following a seminar in November 1991, held as part of the ODA/NAWO Review.

DESPITE ITS CURRENCY and usefulness, the concept of 'sustainable development' lacks precision, is defined in a variety of ways, and is founded on a paradox. Looked at from the standpoint of women's subsistence needs, it seems to suffer from the familiar problem of misplaced universalism; in other words, the assumption of speaking on behalf of 'human features', and global needs as if these were unitary and self-evident. As with the generic use of the term 'mankind', which generalises a dominant position, the idea of sustainability runs the risk of subsuming contradictory interests, based on unequal power, within a value-free and scientifically neutral notion of environmental care.

The conflicting perspectives of North and South in relation to environmental action are already clear, and can be expressed within the terms given by international political discourse. However, the sometimes divergent priorities of men and women with respect to the environment, arising from their different position in the social relations of production, although increasingly the subject of research, are still given insufficient attention within the political and policy domain. The concept of sustainable development must include an understanding of social reproduction as the mutual interaction of gender ideologies and ecological processes if it is to be of any value in enhancing human survival and livelihood.

A perspective on sustainable development that could include this would therefore involve an examination of gender similarities and differences in relation to four key areas:

- rights over the environment;
- energy systems;
- reproductive control;
- epistemologies.

Women's need for access to and rights to use of environmental resources

In different cultural contexts women and men have different relationships to forest, bush, and water resources and different rights over their use. Thus, along with continued attention to the issue of women's land rights must be added a much greater concern with women's declining access to common property resources for food, fuel and fodder, which in some areas account for up to 20 per cent of income, and their use of minor forest products, both domestically and in handicraft production, as an important component of household survival.

Women's labour as an energy system in its own right

In some regions the burden of distance and time imposed on women by ecological impoverishment is reaching the limits of physical endurance and may not be sustainable. Women's labour may no longer be invisible, but is often treated as infinitely expandable. In degraded environments women's own body power is often the only resource left. Yet we still have insufficient knowledge of the space and time changes that are occurring, and their implications for longer-term social reproduction. Women have a disproportionate burden of responsibility for the subsistence and sustainability of their own families, but resources and means at their command are declining. Personal physical degradation and environmental degradation are interconnected.

Women's rights over their own bodies, and their right to resist being used as a resource for others

An emphasis on environmental protection should not be at the cost of an over-simplification of the imperatives of population control. A sustainable approach to population and environment would have to find a way of balancing the conflicting demands of resource provision, environmental protection and reproductive rights. What can be meant by the concept of sustainability if we devote attention to stabilising eco-systems and encouraging their renewability but are still unable even to provide adequate statistics on maternal mortality? Some of the perspectives and strategies advocated for sustainability appear to ignore the social determinants surrounding sexuality and procreation, negating the advances in understanding of the last 15 years. Unequal access to food and medical care endangers women's lives, and the concern with gender and health must be carried forward into discussions of sustainability.

Women's role in local and indigenous knowledge systems

The sustainability debate has drawn attention to the idea of 'loss' and to the biological value of diversity. Epistemological diversity is also important. The devaluation of women's knowledge of habitats, species, medicinal plants, forms of healing, and productive techniques has been documented in a number of cultural contexts. These include not only the suppression of specific forms of ecological knowledge in the South, but also historical accounts of the role and transformation of gender ideology in the development of Western European philosophical and technical systems from the Enlightenment onwards. The sustainability debate questions the absolute pre-eminence of current Western scientific paradigms in relation to agricultural production and the biosphere; it must also consider gender issues in relation to power and knowledge in this context.

Contradictions of sustainability

A 'regenerative' approach to development would need to put these issues at the centre. We cannot create sustainability on the basis of existing gender inequities, because to do so is once again to subsume women's interests under the wider notion of general and, in this case, even global well being.

In some regions the burden of distance and time imposed on women by ecological impoverishment is reaching the limits of physical endurance and may not be sustainable.

Powerful connections: South-South linking

ALAN MACDONALD/GLASGOW HERALD

For the past year and a half Oxfam has funded a South-South linking project for environment and development NGOs. Josefina Stubbs, the project leader based in Oxford, sees a special and integral role for gender in discussion of environment and development. She spoke to GADU about the potential for networks to give women a platform to speak from and to exert influence on decision-making bodies.

We need development which does not look just at women but at everyone, with a gender perspective. Why should women clean up the mess?

Josefina Stubbs

Why should gender, environment and development be considered together?
Gender is an important dimension in environment and development and this must be reflected at various levels of South-South exchanges. It is important to ensure participation by women's organisations because of the work women do. Rural women in the South often have closer contact with the natural environment than do men, and are affected more by the often linked problems of poverty and environmental degradation. Urban women deal directly with the effects of poor sanitation, inadequate housing, and bad transport systems.

An environmental focus for South-South links challenges development models and addresses North-South conflicts. It also makes way for those who want to propose alternative views of 'environment'.

In terms of looking for development solutions to poverty, it must be remem-

bered that in rural communities women and children are usually left behind when men migrate to urban centres. This gives them a greater potential for local leadership. In urban areas women are the majority within popular movements — among the urban poor in Manila and Mexico City, for example — yet in most cases they are not involved in decision making at a level at which conditions are changed. It is now time to recognise this and to take their views into account.

Women of the South generally have a different perspective on the environment than that of local men, or of development experts and visiting environmentalists. Due to the responsibility of defining survival strategies for the household — assigned to women as a consequence of the social division of labour — their daily activities relate to meeting the daily needs of the household: foraging for firewood, fetching water, tilling the land, growing and gathering food. A consideration of women's perspectives, and their objective socio-economic position, will change the focus of the environment-and-development discussion so that it becomes centred on the immediate survival needs, as well as the potential, of the South.

Is there anything special about women and linking?

Linking is an inheritance from women's movements which have centred on networks. But networking does not give the answer on how to integrate gender with more generalised discussions on development and environment. It all depends on how women articulate their needs and priorities within the discussionsto write a new agenda for environment and development. If we do not use networking well we will be ghettoised. NGO networking does not address empowerment or power specifically, although by what it is doing it is challenging the authority of the dominant networks' agenda for environment and development.

How can linking networks help NGOs' work with environment?

Linking is only an appropriate device if it provides access, insights and empowerment. A network, in itself, does not strengthen anything, except perhaps the power of the people who run it. It needs to be used by the participants who have identified the platforms they want access to and the organisations they want to link with.

South-South linking can create new opportunities by giving access to information, ideas and examples to people and organisations. This does not mean that there is a formula. There must be respect for regional and other differences. We cannot use the same strategies everywhere: contrary to the dominant development model of the past, replication does not always work.

The term 'environment', as it is used in the North, has no meaning for most people in the South. Women in particular need to make their own definition. The implicit function of South-South networks is to encourage meetings between representa-

tives of organisations which have a common interest or perspective but which are broad enough to ensure that all legitimate voices are heard. For example the South-South Linking Project will include:

- grassroots communities that are in direct contact with and are directly affected by environmental problems;
- women's organisations that deal with issues related to women and the environment;
- NGOs whose work is centred on local communities and women's groups; and
- government agencies that interact directly with local communities and whose activities are centred on the environment.

Through their participation in these networks women can meet to define the terms of development so that it benefits the environment, as they see it. Within the linking project, regional meetings have been identified as a space where the discussions and conclusions drawn at the country level are to be re-approached from a regional perspective. We expect the regional exchanges to offer the opportunity for women as well as men to decide the actions to be taken. These actions might involve organisations from outside the network.

The presumption has been that organisations in the South are not linked. But they already know each other — a database of 250 NGOs was built up very quickly. The problem with some NGO networks is that they often assume that this relationship is the only one their member organisations have. Networks are much wider and more complex than that, so we need to see linking as a process, not a discrete project.

Should linking be confined to the South?

North-South links are also of value. Environmental degradation is the expression of the wronged relationship between

North and South, and East and West. Much of the decision making is in the North and the South needs access and solidarity to influence these distant decision makers. The environment concerns everyone, so alliances and frank exchanges of information and ideas can not only improve the environmental situation but can contribute to changes in political relationships. This is especially the case for women who have had to suffer the effects of male-dominated development models. As women we are not equal, and we have strong differences; but with a relationship based on recognition of these differences, we can work within our similarities to find a genuine common ground.

Northern women can give support in getting access to the decision makers. For example, Southern organisations need to know how to use the Northern press effectively for their campaigns. Support is needed from Northern women to denounce repression and to show how the real problems are with the North, and that development is not only a Southern problem.

What is being learned from the project?

In the first year of the project questions have arisen about the nature and focus of the linking project itself: Which South are we referring to? What are the levels and entities represented by this project? Who is speaking on behalf of whom? Who is willing to engage in discussions to seek alternative views on environment? All of these questions relate back to basic questions about representation, decision-making and accountability. The main thing that has been learned is that questions still need to be raised, and that more people need to be drawn into the discussion so that their views can be heard.

Josephina Stubbs (standing) *in discussion with some of the facilitators of the Environment Linking project*

JAMES HAWKINS/OXFAM

Resources

TRAINING PACK

Women on earth: gender issues in natural resource management

Irene Guijt

Women, environment, and development links have been the subject of much discussion, and many environmental activities are being undertaken by women, with and without outside support. Much work has also been done in developing clear frameworks for understanding gender dimensions of agriculture and forestry in particular. But these are generally academic approaches and based on formal survey methods, remaining the speciality of academics and policy makers.

Alongside these developments, however, participatory rural appraisal (PRA)[1] methods have seen a dramatic spread and continuous innovation. PRA is an intensive and iterative field-based learning process that uses diagramming by local people as the basis for a semi-structured interviewing approach. The analysis that takes place around these diagrams leads to new insights, by local people and outsiders, about the range of local constraints, potentials and priorities for action.

Although the use of PRA in natural resource management research and projects is widespread, until recently these methods had been little used to provide a gender perspective. Now there is growing appreciation for the way in which they can help in understanding the links between gender issues and natural resource management, but there is very little training material, and most of it is only available in English.

Women on Earth will help fill the existing gap in appropriate training materials by providing a multilingual, audiovisual training package which will merge recent developments in PRA with existing conceptual frameworks to provide a practical and thorough approach to gender analysis in natural resource management. The focus of the material will be to present practical tools, based on PRA principles, that enable fieldworkers to understand gender issues in their work.

The package will comprise a four-part educational video, an optional slide set, and a trainer's guide. The trainer's guide will include a range of training strategies and modules, making it easily adaptable to many training situations at both field and policy levels. The materials will be produced in English, French, and Spanish, and other language versions are being discussed.

The first part of the video will look at how women, environment, and development (WED) issues have been addressed to date, including common misconceptions.

One such misconception typically portrays women as 'wanton destroyers' of the environment, when in fact their decisions and behaviour result from trade-offs relating to the need for survival and self-respect.

This first video will summarise the analytical framework which is illustrated in the other videos. The next three videos will focus on specific case studies, from a range of agro-ecosystems: mangrove vegetation in wetlands in Pakistan, drylands in Burkino Faso, and biodiversity issues in Brazil. Each case will present footage that illustrates a set of problems or misconceptions about gender issues in natural resource management. Each case will also show several research methods in detail. Together, the cases will provide an overview of the key concepts and the practical tools for analysis.

The project pulls together several methodological approaches and the current debate on women and the environment. It will show that gender analysis is essential for the success of any sustainable development initiative, and, more importantly, how to start incorporating it. Another innovation is the participatory video-making process. At three stages in the production, the local collaborating organisations and village women and men will help decide what they want to include in their case study. This video-making process will not only enhance the quality of the materials but will also empower the groups tackling these issues.

The training and filming is to start in December 1992. The training package will be available from August 1993. Provision has been made for the free distribution of a limited number of packs of material to organisations in the South.

For more information contact: Irene Guijt, Sustainable Agriculture Programme, International Institute for Environment and Development, 3 Endsleigh Street, London WC1H 0DD

Unheard Voices: Iraqi women on war and sanctions

Bela Bhatia, Mary Kawar, Marian Shahin from the International Study Team on the Gulf Crisis
CHANGE Thinkbook VIII, 1992

'Wars are made in the minds of men, but they impact on women who have no say in their making.'

'The lives of Iraqi people now take the form of a daily struggle to satisfy basic needs, especially the need for food. Women fare the worst, and Iraqi families owe much to them for their survival.'

Extract from the report.

In the minds of many people the Gulf War finished when the fighter planes stopped dropping their bombs and the media ceased to pay much attention to Iraq. Yet we forget that the burden on Iraqi citizens continues in the form of economic sanctions, bringing about massive inflation rates that make it impossible for many poor families to get by. We also forget that before the Gulf War health and education facilities in Iraq were as high as those in any industrialised nation. The effect of the war and economic sanctions has been to take many parts of Iraq back to pre-industrialised standards.

This new report provides valuable information from inside Iraqi homes on the devastating effects of the war and subsequent economic sanctions on the lives of ordinary Iraqi people, and in particular on Iraqi women. The report is the result of a detailed survey carried out in August and September 1991, in which 80 Iraqi women, mostly married and from poor backgrounds, were interviewd by a team of female researchers. It gives in-depth information and data on the economic, social, and psychological impact of the war and sanctions on the lives of these women. According to the report 80 per cent of women feel that their responsibilities have increased drastically, and 58 per cent claim that their health has deteriorated. These figures are not surprising considering women are facing such adversities as a severe lack of food, fuel and medical supplies due to the sanctions, contaminated water supplies, and damaged sewage systems. It is women who have to search for food and fuel, who have to watch their children die from water-borne diseaes such as typhoid, and who have to take on the added responsibilities of the men they have lost. The report also provides statistics on the income of the families at the time of interview, but oddly enough does not compare these to pre-war incomes.

The scientific material is presented alongside six selected case studies which give personal and touching testimonies of the struggles these women have faced in the post-war period. They talk of how they themselves have had to go hungry in order to feed their families, of stress-induced miscarriages and illnesses, of sewage flooding into their homes; and of lost sons and husbands. One of the women relates her story whilst a baby sits in her lap waiting to be suckled. She is so malnourished herself that her breasts no longer have any milk. Another talks of how most of her family were lost during the war leaving only herself and her daughter. All the women reiterate the point that they felt nothing during the ten-year war with Iran, but that after two months of fighting against the Allies they are 'suffering like never before'.

The words of these women combine with the statistical data to give a shocking account of the experiences of many poor Iraqi women during and after the Gulf War. In the words of one of them: 'All our sufferings are due to the sanctions, sister.

How long will the sanctions continue? We are tired. We are innocent.' This report is unique and important; it contributes to the limited supply of information on the experience of women in situations of war and conflict. Highly recommended reading.

Selma Chalabi

The emancipation of women: An African perspective

Florence Abena Dolphyne
Ghana Universities Press, Accra, 1991

1975 ushered in the UN Decade for Women, which aimed at bringing peace and equality to women the world over. Women from both industrialised and developing nations came together in an effort to articulate their problems and work together in finding solutions. It was during these discussions that Florence Dolphyne became aware that, although women from all societies had a common goal, namely freedom from discrimination within the family structure, employment, and education, there was a clear polarisation of positions held by women from the Western world and women from Africa on how to go about achieving these objectives.

In this slim and readable volume the author clearly lays out an African perspective on the complexities surrounding the emancipation of African women. She outlines various deep-rooted traditional customs, such as polygamy and female circumcision, that stand in the way of emancipation. Whereas many women from the Western world believe that such practices can and should be eradicated by law, the author explains that legislation alone will simply push these practices underground. What is needed is a deeper understanding of why such traditions are maintained and why they have such a strong hold. In the case of female circumcision, for instance, the tradition is so deep-rooted that many women from educated backgrounds who have not been circumcised have undergone the torment of being regarded as unclean by their society. One woman tells of how she was constantly teased by her classmates for not having entered into adulthood. When asked if she was going to circumcise her daughter, she said she would consider it so that her daughter would avoid the ostracisation that she herself had undergone. The author concludes that practices such as female circumcision need to be understood within their cultural context. Only then can effective measures such as education and alternative ceremonies be introduced.

In the second part of the book Florence Dolphyne, who was chairwoman of the Ghana National Council on Women and Development, analyses the effects of the UN Decade for Women on women in Africa. As well as discussing general issues such as education, agriculture, and income generation, she also details the successes and failures of development projects implemented by the NCWD, and draws out the lessons learnt. Finally she discusses the role of NGOs and their contribution to 'women-in-development' activities. She ends by stating that for such activities in Africa to go forward there is an urgent need for women's governmental organisations established during the UN Decade for Women to unite with NGOs towards the common goal of emancipation.

The striking message throughout this book is that the implementation of any educational and development programmes must take into account the cultural values and particular needs of each society if they are to suceed. Although such conclusions are not new, this book is a welcome reminder that cultural contexts must not be overlooked. It is recommended reading for anyone interested in women in the developing world.

Selma Chalabi

Two Halves Make a Whole: Balancing gender relations in development

Produced by CCIC (Canadian Council for International Cooperation), MATCH International Centre, and Comite Quebecois Femmes et Developpement. Available in French and English.

'Development work which does not take into account the needs, interests and constraints of half the population risks major problems with implementation and sustainability... rather like playing in a high stakes game with access to only half the deck.' This manual has three main sections. The first outlines the theory and practice of gender and development, lays out the conceptual toolbox, and discusses the implications and limitations of the GADU approach for organisations at the policy or structural level. The second and third sections are practical, containing sample exercises, module agendas, and case studies for Gender and Development workshops of varying lengths.

The **first section** contains an excellent discussion of different concepts of power. Power-over is what women lack: 'if I have more, you have less'. Alternatives are examined: power-to (solve a problem, learn a skill), power-with (the group), and power-within (self-respect and self-acceptance that gives strength). The writers speak of the need to 'transform our understanding of power, and resist power-over creatively'. Maybe it **can** offer a way forward!

The **second section** contains a number of tools that can guide development work to address gender issues more effectively. Each poses critical questions: on access to and control over resources and benefits, condition and position, level of participation, practical needs and strategic interests. Sara Longwe, a frequent contributor to the GADU Newspack over the years, offers examples of questions to ask about a project's strategy, objectives, management, implementation, and outcome. Other tools include diagrams illustrating the move from WID to GAD, and the difference between practical and strategic interests. A major contribution of this manual to GAD trainers is the section on recurring issues which undermine the legitimacy of the approach. ('It imposes a Western feminist agenda.' 'It is culturally inappropriatge to try to change gender relations through development programmes.') The key approach of consultation with women themselves as the starting point for more equitable development is emphasised.

The **third section** is devoted to case studies. The introduction examines their uses and usefulness, and how they can feed into extended work on project cycles. Some are a few lines in length, to stimulate awareness of whether a project addresses women's practical or strategic interests; on the importance of collecting gender-disaggregated data; on planning and assessment. A key problem for GAD workers is misunderstanding of what the gender and development perspective actually is. The manual opens with a case study called 'What's wrong with this picture?' about an income-generation programme in which male trainers offer workshops to local women entrepreneurs. It is typical of the failure of so many projects, because of its emphasis on the growth of individual income at the expense of the group, rather than addressing women's life situations.

Two halves make a whole is invaluable for anyone realising the importance of gender issues in development work, and looking for the tools. It takes the form of a looseleaf file, and photocopying is encouraged as long as the source is clearly cited. Part of the manual was used in the Women and Development Europe (WIDE) workshop, Dublin, April 1992, and is available from GADU.

Sue Smith

FURTHER READING

Agarwal and Narain (1989) *Village Ecosystem Planning*, London: International Institute for Environment and Development.

Akhter F (1992) *Depopulating Bangladesh, Essays on the Politics of Fertility*, Dacca: Narigrantha Prabartana.

Biehl J (1991) *Rethinking Ecofeminist Politics*, Boston: South End Press.

Boserup E (1989) *Women's Role in Economic Development*, London: Earthscan.

Braidotti R et al (1993) *Women, the Environment and Sustainable Development: Towards a Theoretical Synthesis* London: Zed Books/INSTRAW.

Burkey S (1993) *People First*, London: Zed Books.

Caldwell J (1982) *Theory of Fertility Decline*, London: Academic Press.

Callaway H (1985) *Women Refugees in Developing Countries: Their Specific Needs and Untapped Resources*, Oxford: Refugee Studies Programme, Queen Elizabeth House.

Cecelski E (1987) 'Energy and rural women's work: crisis, response and policy alternatives', *International Labour Review* 126(1):41-64.

Colchester M and Lohmann L (eds) (1992) *The Struggle for Land and the Fate of the Forest*, London: Zed Books.

Commonwealth Expert Group on Women and Structural Adjustment (1989) *Engendering Adjustment for the 1990s*, London: Commonwealth Secretariat.

Commonwealth Secretariat (1989) *Role of Women in Small-scale Fisheries in the South Pacific*, London: Commonwealth Secretariat.

Corpuz V (1992) *Going Back to the Basics: A Feminist Perspective of Sustainable Development in the Philippines*, London: Philippine Resource Centre.

Cross N and Barker R (eds) (1991) *At the Desert's Edge: Oral Histories from the Sahel*, London: Panos Books.

Dankelman I, and Davidson J (1988) *Women and Environment in the Third World: Alliance for the Future*, London: Earthscan.

Davidson J, Myers D with Chakraborty M (1992) *No Time to Waste: Poverty and the Global Environment*, Oxford: Oxfam

Davidson J (1990) *Women and the Environment*, a paper for the Third Meeting of Commonwealth Ministers Responsible for Women's Affairs, Ottawa 1990, Women and Development Programme, London: Commonwealth Secretariat.

DAWN (1988) *Development, Crisis, and Alternative Visions; Third World Women's Perspectives*, London: Earthscan.

Diamond and Orenstein (eds) (1991) *Reweaving the World, The Emergence of Ecofeminism*, Washington DC: Sierra Club Books.

Dinham B (ed) (1991) *The Pesticide Handbook*, London: The Pesticides Trust.

Dinham B (1993) *The Pesticide Hazard: A Global Health and Environmental Audit*, London: The Pesticides Trust/Zed Books.

Drijver C (1990) *People's Participation in Environmental Projects in Developing Countries*, London: International Institute for Environment and Development.

Environmental Liaison Centre (1985) *Women and the Environmental Crisis, A Report on the Proceedings of the Workshops on Women, Environment and Development*, July 1985, Nairobi: Environmental Liaison Centre.

Fox S (1991) *Toxic Work: Women Workers at GTE Lenkurt*, Philadelphia: Temple University Press.

Gassert T (1985) *Health Hazards in Electronics: A Handbook*, Hong Kong: Asia Monitor Resource Center.

Gourlay KA (1992) *World of Waste: Dilemmas of Industrial Development*, London: Zed Books

Gubbels P (1988) 'Peasant farmer agricultural self-development: the World Neighbors experience in West Africa', *ILEIA Newsletter* 4(3):11-14.

Heyzer N (1987) *Women Farmers and Rural Change in Asia*, Kuala Lumpur, Malaysia: Asian and Pacific Development Centre.

ILO (1987) *Linking Energy With Survival*, Geneva: International Labour Office.

ILO (1987) *Women and Land*, Geneva: International Labour Office.

International Policy Action Committee (1991) *World Women's Congress for a Healthy Planet*, Official Report of a Congress held 8-12 November 1991, Miami Florida USA, New York: Women's Environment and Development Organization (WEDO).

IPPF/IUCN/UNFPA (1987) 'Women and the environment' *Earthwatch*, No.37.

IUCN, UNEP and WWF (1980) *World Conservation Strategy*, Gland, Switzerland: International Conservation Union.

IUCN (1987) 'Women and the World Conservation Strategy', *Population and Sustainable Development Programme*, November, Gland, Switzerland: International Conservation Union.

IUCN, UNEP and WWF (1991) *Caring for the Earth*, Gland, Switzerland: International Conservation Union.

Leach M (1992) 'Gender and the environment: traps and opportunities', *Development in Practice*, 2:1.

May N (no date) *No Short Cuts - A Starter Resource Book for Women's Group Field Workers*, London: Change.

Mellor M (1992) *Breaking the Boundaries: Towards a Feminist Green Socialism*, London: Virago.

Mies M and Shiva V (1993) *Ecofeminism*, London: Zed Books.

Ministry of Foreign Affairs, The Netherlands (1989) *Women, Water and Sanitation*, The Hague: Ministry of Foreign Affairs.

Molnar A (1987) 'Forest Conservation in Nepal: Encouraging Women's Participation', *SEEDS*, No 10.

Monimart M (1989) 'Women in the Fight Against Desertification' (a summary), Paris: Organisation for Economic Cooperation and Development.

Moser CON and Peake L (eds) (1987) *Women, Human Settlements and Housing*, London: Tavistock Publications.

Munslow B et al (1988) *The Fuelwood Trap: a Study of SADCC Region*, London: Earthscan.

National Alliance of Women's Organisations, *Women in Development Information Pack*, London: National Alliance of Women's Organisations.

Nayak N (1986) *A Struggle within the Struggle: An experience of a group of women*, Trivandrum, India: Programme for Community Organisations.

OECD (1989) *Focus on the Future: Women and Environment*, London: International Institute for Environment and Development.

Ofofu-Amaah W (1989) *The African Women's Assembly on Sustainable Development*, February, Washington DC: WorldWIDE.

The Pestcides Trust (1989) *The FAO Code: Missing Ingredients*, London: The Pesticides Trust.

Reardon G (1990) *Fisheries Development Programmes in West Africa*, London: Earth Resources Research.

Reynolds F (1989) 'Ecofeminism', *ECOS* 10(2).

Roberts H (ed) (1981) *Doing Feminist Research*, London: Routledge & Kegan Paul.

Rodda A (1991) *Women and the Environment*, London: Zed Books.

Shiva V (1988) *Staying Alive: Women, Ecology and Development*, London: Zed Books; New Delhi: Kali for Women.

Schoeffel P and Talagi S (1989) *The Role of Women in Small-scale Fisheries in the South Pacific*, London: Commonwealth Secretariat.

Sontheimer S (1991) *Women and the Environment, A Reader: Crisis and Development in the Third World*, London: Earthscan.

Starke L (1990) *Signs of Hope: Working Towards Our Common Future*, Oxford and New York: Oxford University Press.

Suliman M (1991) *Alternative Development Strategies for Africa (Vol 2) Environment: Women*, London: Institute for African Alternatives.

Tanzania Women's Magazine (1989) 'Women and Environment Special Issue', September, Tanzania Media Women's Association.

Timberlake L and Thomas L (1990) *When the bough breaks ..., Our Children Our Environment*, London: Earthscan

Transnationals Information Centre (1985) *The Bhopal Papers, Conference Report on the Bhopal Tragedy*, London: Transnationals Information Centre.

UN (1990) 'Women and the Environment, Sustaining Our Common Future', *UN Focus*, May, Geneva: UN Department of Public Information.

Waring M (1989) *If Women Counted: A new feminist economics*, London: Macmillan.

Waterlines, Appropriate Technologies for Water Supply and Sanitation, (Special issue on women as users and managers) Intermediate Technology Publications, Vol 11 No 2, October 1992.

Waters-Bayer A (1986) 'Modernizing milk production in Nigeria: who benefits? *Ceres* 19(5):34-39. (also available in French)

WHO/UNEP (1986) *Pollution and Health*, Geneva: World Health Organisation.

Womankind (worldwide), '*We and the land are one*': *Women and the Environment*, London: Womankind (worldwide).

Women Working Worldwide (1991) *Common Interests: Women Organising in Global Electronics*, London: WWW.

Women in Development Europe (1992) 'Special on Women and Environment', *WIDE Bulletin*, Rome: Women in Development Europe.

Women as Partners in Sustainable Development, ICVA, 1991 Development Forum.

The Women's Environmental Network (1990) *Tissue of Lies? Disposable paper and the environment*, London: WEN

WorldWIDE (1988) *Directory of Women in Environment*, Washington DC: WorldWIDE Network.

WorldWIDE and UNEP (1991) *Success Stories of Women and the Environment: A preliminary presentation in anticipation of the Global Assembly*, Washington DC: WorldWIDE Network.

PERIODICALS

Common Ground, Newsletter on Philippine Environment and Development Action, Philippine Resource Centre, 74-84 Long Lane, London SE1,

EcoForum, Global Coalition for Enviroment and Development, Environment Liaison Centre, Nairobi, Kenya

The ILEIA Newsletter, Information Center for Low-External-Input and Sustainable Agriculture (ILEIA), Kastanjelaan 5, PO Box 64, 3830 AB Leusden, Netherlands, ISSN 0920-8771

New Internationalist, Oxford, UK

News and Views, Women's Environment and Development Organisation, New York, USA

Race Poverty, and the Environment: A Newsletter for Social and Environmental Justice, Earth Island Institute, 300 Broadway, Suite 28, San Francisco, CA 94133-3312, USA

WEDNEWS, Women Environment and Development Network, Environmental Liaison Centre International, Nairobi, ISSN 0250-9989

Women and Rural Development in Africa, Occasional Paper Series, AAWORD/AFARD, BP 3304, Dakar, Senegal

WorldWIDE News, WorldWIDE Network, 1331 H Street NW, Suite 903, Washington DC 20005, USA

News from GADU

1 Africa: how do women cope with drought?

In December 1992, UNIFEM and the Zimbabwe Women's Resource Centre Network organised a meeting on women and drought, attended by 40 national and international NGOs. Three-quarters of the participants were women.

The survival strategies developed by women to cope with the Zimbabwe drought include carpet-making, collecting caterpillars for sale, and gold panning. Malnutrition among adults and low-birth-weight babies indicate a decline in health. Visha, Oxfam's Deputy Country Representative in Zimbabwe, reported that even pregnant and lactating women have participated in food-for-work programmes. A warning was given: neglecting gender in drought response will lead to decreased food production, because food aid and food-for-work programmes have prevented women (who provide 85 per cent or agricultural labour) from carrying out their normal work as food producers.

The group recommended women's involvement in decision making in food-for-work programmes, so that their needs should not be overlooked. A familiar conclusion: let us hope that UNIFEM's plan for a training of trainers in disaster preparedness, with an emphasis on gender, will take it further.

2 South-South learning: Oxfam's work in Asia

AGRA (Action for Gender Relations in Asia) is a forum for Oxfam staff in Asia. The forum meets regularly to exchange and analyse experiences of gender issues. It enables 'gender lead persons' from each of the 15 field offices to share current gender experience in their region with a wider group, and to develop methodologies for integrating gender into development and emergency work. Above all, it provides a focus for the cross-regional experience of gender issues. Conflict, gender and development is the subject of this February's workshop in Thailand for the South-East Asian offices, and offices from South Asia will be discussing gender issues and women's employment at their meeting in Nepal in May.

3 Eurostep meeting on gender-planning methodologies

GADU will be hosting this meeting, to be held in Oxford from 26 to 28 May 1993. The objective will be to exchange experiences amongst several international NGOs in research, evaluation, tools, and strategies; to develop new methodologies emerging from their practice; and document their experience. In the longer term, work is continuing towards ensuring that policy papers issued by the Eurostep network have a gender perspective, and enabling Eurostep to lobby the Development Commission of the European Parliament on gender issues.

4 Tackling violence against women

The National Alliance of Women's Organisations is an umbrella group of UK women's organisations. Its WID (Women in Development) working group, composed mainly of development experts and development-oriented NGOs, meets three times a year to lobby the ODA (UK Overseas Development Administration) on gender.

'Gender-related violence: its scope and relevance' is the title of a paper by Eugenia Piza-Lopez (GADU) and Judy el Bushra (ACORD) recently presented to the ODA. Women experience violence at three levels — the personal, the household, and the public. Gender violence takes many forms — rape and sexual harassment, domestic violence and child abuse, war and exploita-

tion of refugees. It is a human rights issue, and a development issue. It impedes personal development and severely limits the contribution women can make to the lives of those around them. The meeting discussed the definitions of violence in the paper. Getting gender-related violence, so often dismissed as a purely domestic matter, accepted as an issue in public fora is a challenge taken up in the paper's recommendations: action on international legal instruments; bilateral agreements; inclusion of gender-related violence as a criterion in project monitoring and evaluation; and support to women's groups and research centres working on the issue.

5 Linking projects

As part of Oxfam's fiftieth anniversary, GADU is sponsoring a three-year project for women in development to exchange ideas on development practice, to network in the UK and Ireland, to communicate Oxfam's work on gender, and to strategise on gender issues. Several themes have been identified as being of primary concern to women: violence, health and reproductive rights, poverty and sustainable development, and culture.

The project began with a visit to the UK and Ireland of women development workers from the South. The women, hosted in different areas of the UK and Ireland, met with local leaders, trade unionists, and women's groups. They exchanged ideas, shared experiences, and began to develop a methodology for achieving the project's overall objectives.

Preparations are now under way for an international conference on gender and development, and for the South-South exchanges. The aim is to provide fora for Oxfam field staff and Southern women to share practical experiences of working with gender and to develop recommendations, based on the experience of women in the South, for revising and strengthening the policy and practice of development NGOs.